Santa Clara County Free Library

REFERENCE

AN END AND A BEGINNING

AN END AND
A BEGINNING

The South Coast and Los Angeles
1850-1887

Joseph S. O'Flaherty

An Exposition-Lochinvar Book

Exposition Press   New York

EXPOSITION PRESS, INC.

50 Jericho Turnpike   Jericho, New York 11753

FIRST EDITION

LIBRARY OF CONGRESS CATALOG CARD NUMBER: 72-75481

SBN 0-682-47476-2

FOR LOUISE

Contents

PART ONE

PART TWO

PART ONE

CHAPTER 1

"She being fourteen years of age and I, forty"

Mexico ceded Alta California to the United States in the 1848 Treaty of Guadalupe Hidalgo. The transfer of the remote province had little immediate effect on the lives and affairs of its people. However, the discovery of gold in the foothills of the Sierra Nevadas east of what is now Sacramento set in train a world-wide rush to northern California in 1849. The succeeding waves of gold-hungry miners, merchants and settlers quickly submerged the culture and holdings of the Californios in that area.

But in the remote cow counties of southern California, there was little change in the old ways.

In the most noted wedding of the decade, Don Abel Stearns married Arcadia Bandini in May, 1841, at the little church facing the Plaza in Los Angeles. As was customary with the Californios, she retained her full maiden name and added her husband's preceded by "de." Stearns was forty-four. Arcadia Bandini de Stearns was fourteen. The engagement and marriage were subjects of wide interest and gossip. She was a beautiful girl from a prominent and wealthy family marrying a man with a scarred face three times her age. Stearns was most sensitive to the age differential, stating he was forty years old rather than his actual forty-four when he petitioned the prefect of the district regarding marriage proclamations:

> . . . having entered into a marriage contract with Maria Arcadia Bandini with the approval and consent of her father, Don Juan Bandini . . . desiring to avoid the ridicule which the difference

in ages might arouse among thoughtless young people, she being
fourteen years of age and I forty . . . I petition your Worship
graciously to dispense on my behalf with the three proclamations. . . .[1]

Stearns' courtship and marriage of Arcadia meticulously followed the California tradition, although he himself had been
born an American. He, like any Californio in dressing formally,
wore knee breeches with silver-buckled shoes when he met Arcadia at Rancho Jurupa or in Los Angeles. Accompanied by her
dueña, the young girl was dressed demurely in a long silk gown,
usually with short sleeves, and a colored sash around the waist
(corsets had not arrived on the South Coast). Her jewelry was
limited to a gold necklace, earrings of large Baja California
pearls, and a comb in the Spanish tradition in her long hair. An
intricately woven light shawl was thrown around her shoulders
and wrapped around her head while walking. In common with
her friends, she carried a parasol because untanned skin was as
prized here as among the Southern belles of pre-Civil War days.
If Arcadia and Don Abel were riding, with the dueña following
on another horse and the Bandini vaqueros in attendance, she
wore a stiff-brim hat and dressed in pantaloons like her brothers.
When going to the prenuptial bailes, or balls, at the ranchos and
in Los Angeles, Arcadia with her dueña proceeded sedately in
a carreta. This creaking vehicle, rolling on two solid wheels cut
from logs, boasted a canopy and was hauled at a snail's pace by
two oxen. There were no carriages on the South Coast. Don Abel
himself brought the first around the Horn over a decade later.

Preparations for the wedding took weeks, with guests expected
from Santa Barbara to Sonora and Baja California. While the
wedding dress itself was simple in the tradition, elaborate gowns
had to be made for the trousseau and the parties, even though,
as was the custom, Don Abel delivered a wedding gift of three
complete changes of costume well before the wedding date.
Myriad detailed tasks occupied the Bandini household; for example, making quantities of the fragile cascarones which would
be broken over the heads of the guests during the wedding

fandango. Preparing the cascarones was in itself a time-consuming operation. Minute pieces of gilt paper were carefully cut and perfumed. Small holes were drilled in the colored eggs, and the yolks and whites were blown out. The tiny flakes of gilt paper were then laboriously poured into the empty eggshells and the holes sealed with wax.

After an elaborate wedding dinner, the music of the guitars, harps and violins signaled the start of the fandango. By dawn the party was over, and the perfumed gilt flakes of the cascarones were everywhere. However, the fiesta and dancing continued for days, with the young gallants having ample opportunity to show off before the girls their expert horsemanship and left- and right-hand reata work.

Don Abel Stearns built a large single-story adobe home for his bride in Los Angeles at Main and a new street which was called Arcadia, the first of a number of things to be named after her. As with other Californio town houses, the basic house layout was:

> . . . one grand room or sala (in Stearns' house, 100 feet long), flanked by two other rooms, which made up the front of the houses. Two large wings extending back, with rooms generally used as dormitories (bedrooms), and a great high wall in the rear, forming an interior court or square, with wide corridors or verandas on the three sides, both outside and inside generally paved with brick tiles, the same as the floor of the veranda; adobe walls, well whitewashed, with chair-boards around the sala, good and substantial doors and windows, with shutters generally painted green, as were also the cornice and columns supporting the verandas, the whole covered with a flat roof.[2]

Almost immediately the new Stearns' town house—El Palacio de Don Abel as it was generally known—became the center of South Coast society. Stearns obviously enjoyed the ability of his young wife to be a poised and entertaining hostess as she received her guests in the sala, standing by a large square piano under the candle-lighted crystal chandeliers. On at least one occasion, Arcadia Bandini de Stearns needed all of her poise. In the early 1850s she gave a fandango to which some of the more prominent gambling characters of Calle de Los Negros, the notorious gambling and vice street of the town, had not been invited. By midnight of the dance, they reached a decision reinforced by a very substantial quantity of hard liquor. They would invite themselves to the party only two blocks away, in a memorable manner. One of them remembered there was a small cannon with some shot left after the recent war. It seemed an excellent idea to get some black powder, load the cannon and aim it at point-blank range toward the heavy main doors of Stearns' town house where the fandango was in full swing. The cannon was fired, the barrel by some miracle did not burst, and the massive main doors flew open. The music stopped in mid-chord. Armed as always, a number of the guests began shooting at the shadowy forms by the cannon. The Calle de Los Negros group, sobering up somewhat by this time, retreated to a saloon with several wounded to review the situation. Meanwhile, the young hostess told the musicians to resume playing, and the fandango went on for several more hours. Despite the great difference in ages and no children, the Stearns marriage was very much of a success.

A few Americans had settled in southern California during the 1830s and 1840s, men such as Stearns, John Temple, Benjamin D. Wilson and William Workman. All were required to become Mexican citizens. Abel Stearns, after a number of years at sea as a supercargo, had decided to try his fortunes in Mexico and later arrived in Los Angeles, about 1830. He set himself up as a merchant, dealing in hides and tallow as well as furs from American trappers. A few years before his marriage he was seriously stabbed in the face and shoulder in an argument with a sailor over a cask of aguardiente, or brandy. Stearns recovered, but his face was scarred by the wound, which also caused a slight speech impediment.

In the barter economy of the Californios he early recognized the importance of cash. This enabled buying at an advantage and periodically being most helpful to Californio friends who might need money. It was inevitable that he would start buying land. Beginning with Rancho Los Alamitos in 1842, over the years he became the largest landholder on the South Coast. The trading business was highly profitable, and in the course of his dealings he was careful to build up a skein of powerful and lasting friendships with the Californios. In the chaotic administrations of the last Mexican governors, with one coup following another, the few Americans in southern California needed all the friends they could get. Somehow they managed to walk a political tightrope during the emerging war between Mexico and the United States, and were ready to participate in the cattle prosperity of the Californios.

CHAPTER 2

"Bring me five or six pounds of lead"

Only five years after Mexico had ceded Alta California to the United States, Don Juan Capistrano Sepulveda was able to shout at a magnificent Fourth of July party and ceremony on the South Coast: "Viva los Estados Unidos! Viva Mexico! Somos Amigos!"[1] His Californio friends could heartily second the toast. During the years after the Gold Rush, cattle could be sold on the hoof at high prices in the San Francisco and Sacramento areas. Eighty million dollars of gold were taken out of the Sierra foothills of northern California in 1852. One hundred thousand miners crisscrossed over a 2000-square-mile area while working in the mud and sleeping in leaky cabins or tents. Their food came into the hills by mule-pack train. Beef was at a premium and such luxuries as potatoes sold for as much as forty cents a pound at the mining camps.

Tens of thousands of cattle were driven north from the South Coast by the Californios. These drives covered a distance of four to five hundred miles over extremely rugged and barren country. A herd of a thousand cattle would be more than a month on the trail, driven by a trail boss and four or five vaqueros. The drives started after the first heavy rain in the fall and continued through April. The routes up the coast included stretches of splashing through the surf above San Buenaventura and climbing trails across the Tehachapi Mountains. Cave J. Couts sent a message south in 1852 covering some of the problems of a cattle drive:

> The cattle and the horses are getting on well. The nest of thieves in the Sta. Clara did all they knew to make me lose a lot, if not all. By believing all they told me to be false and

threatening a couple pretty closely, I escaped. I learned they got about 100 head of Forster, 50 from Jose Anto. Arguello, 70 of Machados, all of Castros, and others in proportion. I have not had an opportunity of counting since leaving Triumpho Rancho, but have lost very few if any—have had no kind of stampede and no kind of bad luck.[2]

Cout's particular drive was successful. But as he indicated, others were not. Vaqueros were killed by outlaws, sometimes being lassoed from their horses to be murdered at leisure. Stampedes were common; stock would be lost in great fields of mustard growing to the height of a man on horseback; cattle would go lame; and lack of grass and water was a continual hazard. With the prevailing rich prices for cattle and superbly trained Californio horses, the number and organization of Indian raids increased to the extent that the southern California frontier and the trail routes north were on an almost continuous alert basis. As Lewis Granger wrote Abel Stearns in 1851: "News has reached us that the Tulare Indians have killed Dalton's party and Capt. Dorsey's party. . . . Thirteen men in all have been reported to be massacred."[3] Or as John M. Bright after repeated Indian attacks wrote in a letter published in the Los Angeles *Star* in 1856: ". . . Uncle Davy Smith is going to start for Los Angeles in the morning with a letter from the miners at Kern River to the Sheriff of Los Angeles, to raise a company to come to their assistance. If you come up, I want you to bring me five or six pounds of lead."[4]

The Indian raids into the South Coast were down the Cajon or San Gorgonio passes. During the 1850s the raiding parties were Utes and Southern Paiutes, as well as the Hamakhavas from the Colorado River. The Tulares, along with some former mission Indians, raided from the southern end of the San Joaquin Valley across the Tehachapis and through San Fernando Pass. With the approach of the monthly full moon, the ranchos braced for attacks which could extend to the haciendas of the ranchos themselves. Ute Chief Cuaka may have actually boasted that the ranchos were kept as stockraisers for his benefit.

The Californios fought back in a series of little-known skir-

mishes and bloody episodes which equaled or exceeded those
in other parts of the American West. After Ute attacks on Rancho
Azusa, Abel Stearns headed a Californio posse which fought a
vicious running battle with the Indians retreating through Cajon
Pass. Seventeen were killed in the engagement, two of them
Californios. In another skirmish it was only good fortune that
the following posse was not massacred to a man:

> The Utahs have been in the valley within a week past, and
> drove off all of Jose Maria Lugo's caballada, amounting to
> seventy-five horses. Fifteen men . . . started in pursuit, came
> upon the Utah 100 miles from the Cajon Pass, attacked them,
> but were repulsed with the loss of one man, a Sonoran who
> fell at first fire, pierced with five balls. Had it not been for the
> darkness of the night, the party in pursuit would have been
> all killed, as the Utahs were fifty strong, armed with rifles and
> revolvers.[5]

Even more serious than the persistent Indian raids was a
continuing increase in gangs of drifters from the gold fields,
hangers-on in San Francisco and the Californio's own castoffs.
Initially, they smelled the gold to be gotten for cattle and horses
but soon expanded their activities into robbery, pillage and
casual murder. Jack Powers, Salomon Pico and Joaquin Murieta
headed some of the notorious robber bands. Murieta was finally
run down in Pacheco Pass east of Gilroy in 1853.

Stealing of seven horses eventually resulted in one of the
most extensive outlaw hunts in California history, in late January
and February of 1857. A wild young man of twenty-one was
sent to the new state prison at San Quentin for the theft in early
1856. Juan Flores, member of a well-known Californio family
in the Santa Barbara area, promptly started a prison breakout
with a fellow inmate, Pancho Daniel. Flores' and Daniel's escape
plans worked, and the two set up a robber base in the Santa
Ana Mountains on the South Coast. It was not that difficult to
assemble a gang called the Manilas (a variation of "handcuffs").
The Manilas went into the business of robbing stagecoaches
and pack trains, as well as rustling cattle and horses. However,

the taking over the mission town of San Juan Capistrano and casually murdering a small merchant, George W. Pflugardt, finally triggered the South Coast into action against them. Juan Forster, whose home was at the old mission, sent a scared boy galloping on horseback and spreading the word as he went to Forster's brother-in-law, Don Andres Pico, and Sheriff James R. Barton in Los Angeles. While Forster and the nearby ranchos braced themselves for outlaw attack, both Sheriff Barton and Andres Pico moved into action. Barton raised a posse of six men, including himself, William H. Little, Charles K. Baker, Frank H. Alexander, Charles F. Daly and Alfred Hardy. The posse headed for Capistrano, stopping at Rancho San Joaquin, some eighteen miles from the mission town, to rest and feed their horses. Meanwhile, Andres Pico began systematically mobilizing Californio and ranger forces, as well as sending a rider to Fort Tejon for calvary support.

Don Jose Andres Sepulveda at Rancho San Joaquin warned Sheriff Barton that the Manilas under Flores and Daniel could number as many as fifty well-armed men. He also emphasized that the ranchos were organizing for defense, not attack, until Pico could assemble some forces. Information had come from Forster indicating he felt the Capistrano mission could be held for a while unless the outlaws made an all-out assault. Further, the Indians under Chief Manuelito were not supporting the Manilas, and their scouts would keep the gang under surveillance. Sheriff Barton, a brave but brash man, told Sepulveda he could handle the gang and ordered his men to saddle up.

The posse rode into an ambush about twelve miles from the rancho near the present town of Irvine. Baker, ahead on scout with Little, was the first to be shot from the saddle. Barton and the other three galloped up, firing at a group of about twenty men scattered in the barranca by the side of the trail. The Sheriff, Little and Daly were cut down. Somehow, Hardy and Alexander were able to break out of the encircling outlaws and race for Rancho San Joaquin. "For the first 400 yards of the chase, the balls whistled thick and fast around the fugitives, making the dust on the road fly up before and around them."[6] They made it, and the shock of the ambush spread throughout the South Coast. A heavily armed fourteen-man party with four coffins left Los Angeles to pick up the dead. "Barton's body had three wounds in the region of the heart, the left arm broken, and a shot in the right eye. Baker was shot in the back of the head when aiming at Flores, also in the right eye and cheek. Daly shot in the mouth and body. The face burned with powder. The bodies had evidently been fired upon after death."[7]

The mutilation of the bodies was a small but final ingredient solidifying the public determination to track down the gang at any cost. The bandits, Juan Flores and Pancho Daniel, found there was little support for them from the Californios on the South Coast, in sharp contrast to the experience of Tiburcio Vasquez some years later. Cavalry detachments were sent into the area from Fort Tejon and San Diego while the Californios had organized under Don Andres Pico. Mounted ranger bands fanned out from Los Angeles, El Monte and San Bernardino. Chief Manuelito's braves were used as scouts.

In small groups the bandits were killed or captured. Flores was taken once with two companions and escaped. Andres Pico, who was deadly in his pursuit of the gang, on hearing of Flores' escape solved any possible security problem with the two gang members his party had just picked up. He hanged them about two miles south of what is now Irvine Park. Pico then split his forces and continued sweeping the area. Flores was finally taken by Army troops patrolling Simi Pass at the western end of San Fernando Valley. Two of the gang got as far as San Buenaventura, where, captured after a gun battle, they were promptly hanged. Flores was brought to Los Angeles. A hastily convened public meeting gave a shouted verdict, and the young bandit was hustled up to Fort Hill behind the jail to a temporary gallows.

While the whole town watched, Alfred Hardy, one of the two survivors of the posse, placed the noose around Flores' neck, and the hanging rope was William Little's lariat.

The plank was pulled, but the fall was too short. Flores strangled to death.

Pancho Daniel, the other gang leader, got through the guarded mountain passes and was finally captured, wearing Sheriff Barton's silver- mounted belt, in San Jose. He was returned to Los Angeles and lynched. Only one man of the entire gang, Luciano Tapia, was legally tried and charged with the murder of George W. Pflugardt, the Capistrano merchant. He was found guilty and hanged.

The Californio skirmishes with the Indians and outlaw bands at the best could only be defensive. It was impossible to provide any effective protection to the cattle herds scattered over hundreds of thousands of acres of range. The main rancho building, or hacienda, was usually designed as a potential small fort for the protection of the rancho people. As the raids increased during the 1850s, the train of horses (caballada) and some of the cattle-breeding stock were put in a protected pasture near the hacienda. The pasture was surrounded by an adobe wall capped by skulls of cattle with the long, curving steers' horns interlaced. With measures like these and in spite of the increased volume of raids, the herds continued to expand.

CHAPTER 3

"A veritable fortune
of gold slugs wrapped
in a large handkerchief"

The long-horned black cattle of the ranchos weighed 600 to 800 pounds, considerably smaller and lighter-boned than the range stock of later years. About ten acres of land was required for each head of stock, and other than extreme drought years, the herds flourished. There were no fences, and barbed wire was not generally available until the mid-seventies. The semi-wild cattle were rounded up for branding and tallying in the late spring or summer.

Because of their size, each rancho would have as many as a half dozen different roundup locations or rodeos. Strays or mavericks and their calves became the property of the Californio holding the rodeo. As the ranges were unfenced and herds intermingled, an important appointed municipal official—the Judge of the Plains—had jurisdiction over each rodeo. His function was to interpret traditional rules and settle arguments on the spot. It was a responsible and prestigious position in a cattle economy, with full-grown steers in the 1850s worth thirty dollars a head in gold at the rodeos. Hot-tempered men could readily start disputes which would end in bad blood or worse. As a result, respected Californios such as Don Antonio Maria Lugo were expected to, and did, serve for years as Judges of the Plains.

Complicating the roundup and oftentimes requiring special roundups was the southern California wild mustard. To outlanders it was almost unbelievable to see it stretching for miles on the plains and hills. The mustard shot up after the winter rains, with the largest stalks towering to eight feet in height, capped with heavy yellow blooms. In the summer the thick brittle stalks formed a miniature dry jungle which made a perfect hiding place for cattle. In the worst areas the Californios would organize a joint roundup effort from neighboring ranchos for "a run through the mustard." The head-high mustard was well remembered by the American sailors and marines when their column was moving on foot from San Pedro in their attack on Los Angeles in 1846. They discovered the defending Californios at Rancho San Pedro had made many runs through the mustard. The end result was that the small invading column fell back to the U.S.S. *Savannah* anchored a mile or so off Rattlesnake (Terminal) Island and buried their dead on Dead Man's Island.

Wild horses as well as cattle flourished on the hills and plains of southern California. The original horse stock had been brought from Mexico, with the basic blood lines being Spanish-Arabian. Spain's conquest of Mexico had introduced horses to the New World. After the colonization of Alta California, the herds of wild strays had grown at an almost incredible rate during the ensuing seventy-five years. Periodically, a rancho would have a recogida, or horse roundup, to fill out the domestic herd or simply to slaughter the wild horses to save the range for the cattle.

The Californio and his vaquero spent much of their lives in the saddle. As would be expected, the large caballada or rancho herd of horses, was meticulously trained for work with the cattle. Horace Bell was impressed with the sorting-out work at rodeos:

> All of this work must be done inside of two days, as during the time, this great herd has no food, and may become maddened from hunger and thirst. To penetrate this formidable body . . . is a delicate and dangerous operation, but to see how the vaqueros do it, their perfection of horsemanship, the adroitness with which they apply the reata, the cleverness and ease with which they extricate a cow and her calf from this living labyrinth, excites one's admiration to the highest degree.[1]

The toughness and durability of the Californio horses and their riders could be exaggerated but not by a great deal. Upon hearing of the sudden illness of their elderly father, Don Jose Andres Sepulveda (who was nearly sixty himself at the time) saddled up and, together with his brother, covered forty-two miles from his hacienda at Rancho San Joaquin to Los Angeles in considerably less than three hours. This time record included fording three rivers shortly after the end of the spring rains.

The haciendas at San Joaquin and the neighboring Canada de Santa Ana were typical of the outlying ranchos. The main building was a defensive rectangular or square unit surrounding a large courtyard. Parts of the building might be two stories, with the walls of adobe (clay bricks dried in the sun and usually twelve inches square and four inches thick). The walls would be two or three bricks deep, with loopholes let into the walls for rifle fire. The flat roof was covered with asphaltum (la brea) or was of tile. Tile was preferred by the 1850s in the outlying areas because of fire arrows which had ignited a number of tar roofs during the increased Indian and outlaw attacks.

The hacienda might have as many as thirty rooms, not including a harness shop, a shoemaker's room and the like. The rooms opened on a covered verandah into the courtyard, which could be a half acre or more in extent. Outside the heavy courtyard gate were rows of small adobe houses for the Indian members of the large headquarters establishment. Adjacent to the main building were a vineyard, a kitchen garden, some acreage devoted to corn and wheat and very often orange and olive groves.

Rancho Canada de Santa Ana consisted of several hundred people. In addition to the large Yorba family, according to Don Meadows, there were " . . . four wool-combers, two tanners, one butter and cheeseman who directed every day the milking of from fifty to sixty cows, one harness maker, two shoemakers, one jeweler, one plasterer, one carpenter, one majordomo, two errand boys, one sheepherder, one cook, one baker, two washerwomen, one woman to iron, four sewing women, one dressmaker, two gardeners, and a man to make the wine. . . . More than a hundred lesser employees were maintained on the rancho. . . . Ten steers a month were slaughtered to supply the hacienda."[2]

Soapmaking was typical of the wide variety of routine tasks that were part of rancho life. It was begun by placing a huge boiler on top of a furnace loaded with chunks of wood. The boiler, perhaps ten feet deep and wide, with the upper part of wood, was filled with tallow and the fattest portions of beef. Some water was added, and the mixture was tried out. The grease was then dipped into a large wooden box. Lye, made from mineral earth mixed with ashes, was dumped into the grease and stirred in. Finally, the mixture was boiled, and a very white soap was the result.

Rancho life started at dawn. This applied to the master as well as the vaquero. The morning meal was coffee or thick sweet chocolate with a tortilla or perhaps a dish of pinole (a gruel of ground corn). Depending on the time of year, the principal meal was at noon or in the evening. It began with soup thickened with rice or dumplings. The main course consisted of fresh or dried beef (often in a highly flavored stew with vegetables, including tomatoes), chicken or fish. The side dishes were frijoles (beans), fresh vegetables from the kitchen garden and tortillas. The vaqueros and the children used a rolled-up tortilla as a spoon for the stew or frijoles, with part of the tortilla spoon eaten with the dipped food. Dessert was cheese and fruit accompanied by the usual coffee or chocolate. There were few pastries, as sugar had traditionally been scarce and expensive. Wine was used sparingly; aguardiente was an after-dinner drink, and for the young bucks and fiestas. Oddly enough, pork, mutton, deer or bear meat was not popular with the Californios.

There was plenty of tallow-candle light (along with the smell that went with it) during and after the evening meal. With burgeoning families, visiting relatives and welcomed travelers, it was a wonderfully close-knit society. The rancho establishment lived well and ate well, including the former mission Indians.

The rancho system was built on Indian labor. It still retained
much of the paternal but less of the rigorous supervision of the
mission priests years earlier.

In the name of progress the initial government decrees "sec-
ularizing" the California missions were issued in 1826 and 1831,
a few years after Mexico won her independence from Spain.
The result of the decrees, whether intended or not, was to lay
open for the takers the land, buildings, livestock, and above all
the lives of several tens of thousands of converted Indians (neo-
phytes) who lived and worked in the mission establishments.
Most of the famous Mexican land grants made by the governors
of the province to deserving supporters were spoils of the "secularization" decrees. The tragedy was the thousands of mission
Indians who were summarily scattered with the wind after
several generations of formidable but orderly mission life. Some
of them returned to the remnants of their original villages; some
went beyond the southern California frontier to the Owens and
Mojave river regions; many became part of the ranchos; and a
large remainder drifted into and around Los Angeles and the
other small towns. The rancho life for the Indians in the main
was good. Intermarriage had never been discouraged under the
Spanish colonizing tradition, and the highly skilled vaquero and
rancho artisan positions provided adequate job opportunities.

However, many of the former mission Indians as the years
went by ended up in a position of unofficial and informal slavery.
As the Indians near the little towns became increasingly degraded, they were considered scarcely human and a serious nuisance, as the Los Angeles *News* said in a descriptive piece
of writing: ". . . Decay and extermination has long since
marked them for their certain victims. . . . Their scanty earnings
at the end of the week are spent for rum in the lowest purlieus.
. . . They have filled our jails, have contributed largely to the
filling of our state prison, and are fast filling our graveyards,
where they must either be buried at public expense or be per-
mitted to rot in the streets and highways. . . . "[3]

The manager, or majordomo, of Rancho Los Alamitos sent
an 1852 letter to Don Abel Stearns in Los Angeles: "I wish you

would deputize someone to attend the auction that usually takes place on Monday and buy me five or six Indians. . . . "[4] He was writing Stearns about the weekly Indian auctions. Again, quoting the Los Angeles *News* on this practice: "For years past it has been the custom of those most extensively engaged in the cultivation of the soil, to hang around the Mayor's court on Monday morning and advance the degraded Indian a few dollars with which to pay his nominal fine for having been dragged through the streets to the station house in a state of beastly intoxication. . . . "[5]

According to Horace Bell: "They could be sold for a week, and bought up by the vineyard men and others at prices ranging from one to three dollars, one-third of which was to be paid to the peon at the end of the week, which debt due for well-performed labor would invariably be paid in aguardiente (the cheapest and rawest grape brandy), and the Indian would be happy until the following Monday morning."[6]

Under this procedure, the Indian problem around the small southern California towns did not last too many years. The Indians died.

John G. Downey, later governor of California at age thirty-two, ran a drugstore in Los Angeles in the cattle-boom years of the early 1850s. The store had a safe. There were no banks. Downey usually had $200,000 of his Californio friends' and customers' money in his custody. As he described it: "Each depositor put in his sack or bag of buckskin, filled with gold dust or fifty dollar octagonal slugs, tied with a string, and took no receipt. When he wanted money, he called for his bag, took out what he wanted and put it back again."[7]

The Californios could afford to be casual about money when cattle on the hoof got as high as seventy-five dollars a head delivered in San Francisco. Even on the ranchos the price of a full-grown steer rose to thirty to forty dollars—perhaps eight times the price of a few years before. The Californios spent the money as rapidly as did some overnight oil millionaires on the South Coast several generations later.

Prior to the Gold Rush and the Mexican-American war, a cattle hide was the medium of exchange for the Californio. Known to the Americans on both coasts as leather dollars or California banknotes, hides, along with tallow, were used to barter for the few luxuries and essentials carried by the trading ships anchored in the open roadsteads off San Pedro and San Juan Capistrano. All of this changed with the booming cattle prosperity. The Californio had hard money for the first time. He spent it as rapidly as it came in, and the money moved out of the South Coast. Little was invested in savings, irrigation or stock improvement. Financial planning was negligible, and the Californio with his large family and numerous relatives quickly adjusted to and speedily exceeded the new cash income. Concurrent with this was the steadily increasing cash burden for land and water litigation initiated by the Gold Rush. The Californio's answer to any temporary cash shortage was simple. He borrowed money from the local Americano merchants. In an isolated economy like the South Coast of the period with no banking system, there was only a very limited amount of loanable money. As a result, the interest rates were enormous. Typical was the case of Don Jose Ramon Yorba, who mortgaged 17,000 acres of Rancho Las Bolsas along with his hacienda for $5500 at an interest rate of 5 per cent a *month*. But to Yorba and the other Californios there was no problem, with cattle prices setting new highs in San Francisco.

Young newcomers to the South Coast in the 1850s like Horace Bell and Harris Newmark were awed by the extravagance of the Californios with their new-found wealth. Saddles were trimmed with solid silver; spurs were gold; bridles had silver chains. Newmark estimated Don Antonio Maria Lugo's horse gear cost $1500. A suit of clothes for a caballero might cost $500 to $1000. General Mariano Vallejo after the Gold Rush got in the habit of flinging "the boy who held his horse an ounce of gold, equivalent to sixteen dollars."[8]

The Californio ladies went in for costly rugs, four-post bedsteads and quantities of intricate foreign lace. They bought expensive tortoise-shell combs and huge quantities of massive silk and satin gowns.

The young men speedily developed an appetite for high-stakes gambling. The professional card sharps from San Francisco who smelled easy money were happy to oblige.

Above all, the Californios liked betting and horse racing. In the 1850s they had the cash to bet as well as land, horses and cattle of former days. When Don Jose Andres Sepulveda bought an Australian horse called Black Swan, it was inevitable that he would be challenged by Don Pio Pico, the last Mexican governor of California, with his proven local favorite, Sarco. At least $50,000 in gold, land, horses and cattle was bet on the race in 1852. The Sepulvedas had been losing to the Picos rather consistently. This time they were convinced that they would win. Jose Andres Sepulveda's wife "was driven to the scene of the memorable contest with a veritable fortune of gold slugs wrapped in a large handkerchief."[9] Her servants scattered through the crowd taking bets on Black Swan. It was evident that the Sepulvedas had given considerable forethought to the race. At the last moment they brought out Black Swan's rider. He was a very small Negro dressed like a jockey of another generation and had been imported for the occasion. His saddle was the stripped-down English type as contrasted to the heavy California saddle of Pico's horse, Sarco. The nine-mile course was out San Pedro Road in Los Angeles to a pole at the four-and-one-half-mile mark and return. Black Swan won by four and a half lengths. The light jockey and the saddle made the difference.

While it lasted, the Californios had a magnificent spree. Unfortunately for them the lucrative selling prices for cattle on the hoof in San Francisco and Sacramento had not gone unnoticed. Texas herds began to arrive in northern California after being driven 1500 or 2000 miles over a "trail of dangers and uncertainties—long dry drives that set the cattle mad with thirst and drew saddle horses to 'skin and bones'; alkaline lakes that poisoned and killed thirsting herds; malpais ridges that cut hoofs to the quick and set the riders afoot; and the eternal threat of loss to white and Indian thieves."[10]

Notwithstanding the obstacles, thousands of Texas cattle survived the drives, and other thousands arrived from the Missouri frontier. This influx was further supplemented by young herds in the San Joaquin Valley. Large flocks of sheep moved into the booming northern California markets from New Mexico, as well as from new sheep ranches in Monterey County.

The result was inevitable. Cattle prices dropped sharply in a market becoming saturated, and in 1855 the fall was accelerated by forced sale of South Coast cattle because of a drought. By the next year the beef market was glutted. Full-grown steers were selling for less than half the price of several years earlier. The Los Angeles *Star* of April 26, 1856, reflected the prevailing feeling on the South Coast: "The flush times are passed—the days of large prices and full pockets are gone."[11] The *Star* neglected to mention that the Californios' mortgages with the fantastically high interest rates were still there, along with litigation over land boundaries and titles.

CHAPTER 4

"There were no surveyors in this country, and fortunately no lawyers"

The Gold Rush had made the Californios of the South Coast rich for a while. But it also brought in a horde of miners and settlers to northern California who beheld the vacant lands around San Francisco and Sacramento with hungry eyes. Even superficial investigation showed them a maze of land titles and riparian law problems which the settlers or squatters were prepared to exploit to the maximum. At the time, the newcomers had little interest in the rancho lands of the remote cow counties of southern California. However, it was inevitable that the South Coast lands would come under the same pressure and scrutiny.

The Treaty of Guadalupe Hidalgo of 1848 stated that the Californios would be "admitted . . . to the enjoyment of all the rights of the United States according to the principles of the Constitution; and . . . shall be maintained and protected in the free enjoyment of their liberty and property."[1] Unfortunately, the treaty makers did not conceive of the impact of the Gold Rush on the yet-to-be-born state of California and the increase in value of lands with questionable titles and boundaries under American law. As Robert G. Cleland summarized it:

> . . . titles to many California grants, owing to lost or defective documents, haphazard surveys, poorly defined boundaries, and unfulfilled conditions, were technically imperfect even under Mexican law, and therefore legally subject to forfeiture. Among the grants were mission lands, pueblo lands, private lands and public lands; titles technically complete and titles technically faulty; titles granted in good faith and titles granted solely to anticipate American annexation; titles free from any shadow of suspicion and titles obtained through obvious fraud.[2]

There was no question that the land-title maze had to be resolved over a period of time if for no other reason than the large number of heirs of the Californios themselves. It was equally true that the Federal Government was forced and lobbied to precipitous action with the flood of newcomers to northern California. The result was the United States Land Commission established by Congress in 1851. This three-man commission was to sit in San Francisco for three years (later extended) to review all California titles held under Mexican or Spanish grants. Provision was made for appeal to the Federal courts. The Board of Land Commissioners soon found that it had a major task.

The commissioners discovered that boundary descriptions of the Californios' ranchos made interesting reading and not much more. A Señor Guirado prepared and authenticated this description of Rancho Las Bolsas in 1834:

> The cord was stretched toward the north thirty degrees east from the seashore past a hill near a cienega (marsh) where there are two willow trees of the same size for a distance of 9440 varas (this beginning was on the shore near Sunset Beach), then to some prickly-pear (cactus) trees on a sand hill where a cross was placed, then taking a direction to the east 5500 varas were counted to an alder tree with green shoots, then taking a direction east two degrees south we measured 4160 varas, terminating at the old bed of the Santa Ana River where we placed a landmark on a cottonwood tree, from which we broke off some branches to distinguish it, then varying the direction and going toward the south along the old river bed for a distance of 14,250 varas to the seashore where a landmark was placed, then to conclude the measurements we measured along the beach 19,000 varas to the point where the measurements commenced, by which was concluded the measurements to the satisfaction of all the interested parties, and I so sign with three of my assistants, according to law.
>
> Rafael Guirado, May 22, 1834.[3]

One would suspect that a number of these markers might disappear over the years, particularly as the three main South Coast rivers had a marked propensity for changing their courses.

Disheartening as the Las Bolsas description was to the American surveyors in later years, the method of measuring distance and precise direction introduced even more variables. A 50-vara or perhaps a 130-vara rawhide reata was attached to two stakes or lances by the vaqueros. This was a surveyor's chain, with a vara being approximately one yard. The rawhide reata's length was examined and accepted by the magistrate responsible for the land measurement. The measurements began with one vaquero mounted on horseback holding the stake at the starting point, with the other riding or galloping off until he reached the end of the reata. A tally was made, and the procedure was repeated. There was no allowance for the stretching of the reata or the fact that the riders were going in much more than in the general direction of the next reference point.

Don Juan Bandini's reply in 1855 to the casualness of land titles along with their description and measurement was to the point when he wrote in the *Southern Californian* of April 11, 1855:

> In the examination of our land titles, no attention has been paid to the usages and customs of the country, nor much less to the investigation of whether defects in some of the requisite forms may have proceeded from bad faith on the part of the grantees, or from want of knowledge on the part of the officers whose business it was to have acted in conformity to the provisions of the laws. It is evident that the colonization laws had for their object the settlement of a country lying waste. . . . There were no surveyors in the country, and fortunately no lawyers. Judges were not professors of law; every transaction was executed in simplicity and good faith. . . .[4]

Juan Bandini's contention that every land transaction of the Californios was executed in simplicity and good faith was certainly open to considerable question, as exemplified by the long feuds both within and between the Dominguez and the Palos Verdes branche of the Sepulveda family. To a greater or lesser extent, aspects of the Dominguez-Sepulveda controversies applied to all of the rancho families of the South Coast.

Juan Jose Dominguez was a soldado de cuera, or leather-jacket soldier, of New Spain. Of Catalonian descent, Dominguez was typical of the breed of men who served in the Spanish armies on the outlying borders of their country's new possessions. After retiring from the military service in 1782 he decided to settle in the new pueblo whose name had speedily been abbreviated in common usage to Los Angeles from El Pueblo de Nuestra Senora, la Reina de Los Angeles, de Porciuncula. Two years later Juan Jose Dominguez was given a permission to use over 75,000 acres of land south of the pueblo's own holdings at what is now near Rosecrans Boulevard extending from the Los Angeles River to the Pacific Ocean west and south, including the Palos Verdes Peninsula. He called his permission Rancho San Pedro. At his death in 1809 he willed his holdings to his brother, Cristobal, another leather-jacket soldier. Cristobal did nothing for nearly ten years to affirm his claim on Rancho San Pedro. Meanwhile, Juan Jose's executor, Manuel Gutierrez, settled the estate's debts and moved onto the rancho. Shortly thereafter, Jose Dolores Sepulveda began grazing stock on the Palos Verdes segment of the rancho, presumably after having paid Gutierrez for the land. Similarly, Augustin Machado and the Avila brothers occupied other portions of the rancho.

Finally, in 1817, Cristobal Dominguez took action on Rancho San Pedro. Governor Sola in 1822 affirmed his petition, and the ayuntamiento, or common council, of Los Angeles was directed to carry out the decree and establish the boundaries of Rancho San Pedro. The survey was completed, and the pueblo's records reflected Cristobal's title. However, the Sepulvedas and the others continued to occupy the land as Jose Dolores Sepulveda rode north to Monterey to plead their case with the governor. While returning to Los Angeles he made a stop at the Mission de la Purisima Concepcion, north of Santa Barbara. In one of the rare mission Indian uprisings he was killed during the night. Sepulveda's death, leaving his widow and five small children, further delayed resolution of the rancho dispute.

It fell to Cristobal Dominguez's twenty-year-old son, Manuel, as head of the family, to take over in 1823 the rancho fight from his ailing father, who died two years later. Jose Loreto and

Juan, the two oldest Sepulveda children, were eight and nine at the time. However, they had strong friends in Manuel Gutierrez, who believed he owned Rancho San Pedro, and in their relatives who had Rancho San Joaquin and Rancho San Vicente. Gutierrez aggressively expanded his herds on the rancho to the point that "every cow was followed by five calves of the Gutierrez brand, and every mare by three colts."[5] Not only did he establish a reputation as an able ranchero, but he served as a respected Judge of the Plains and was Primero Alcade, or Mayor, of Los Angeles. The twenty-year-old Manuel Dominguez had formidable adversaries.

The Dominguez family settled on the hill named after it at Rancho San Pedro in 1825. Manuel, other than being a son of a leather-jacket soldier, had no prestige or money to defend his title to the rancho lands. His first move was a happy one on several counts. He fell in love with, and married two years later, Maria Engracia Cota. Her father was the local commissioner of the Mexican government and allied with the powerful Nieto family, whose lands bounded Rancho San Pedro on the east. Almost immediately after his marriage, with the support of the Cotas and Nietos he moved into local politics and by 1832 was Primero Alcade himself.

As a local political figure it was clear to Manuel that the Sola decree awarding the lands to the Dominguezes was tenuous at the best with the turbulent politics of the Alta California province. It was equally clear to him as the years went by that the rancho lands occupied a prime strategic location in the development of the South Coast. With his father-in-law's support he obtained another shaky political decree in 1828 ordering the removal of the Sepulveda and Machado herds. When the ayuntamiento sent five men to help Dominguez carry out the decree, there was a solid block of well-organized support for the Sepulvedas and the Machados, as the enforcement officer sadly reported: " . . . a superior force was found on the said Rancho that made opposition. I hope Your Honor will render me the necessary assistance in order that my decrees will be executed and not laughed at."[6] The assistance requested by the conscientious official was not forthcoming. The status quo continued for another six years, with Manuel Dominguez systematically building his own alliances.

Both sides felt that the new governor, Jose Figueroa, would be responsive to their claims. By this time, Jose Loreto Sepulveda was nineteen and the head of the family, while his brother, Juan Capistrano, was twenty. In an 1834 arbitration ruling, Governor Figueroa sustained the Dominguez claim over Gutierrez but awarded Palos Verdes to the Sepulvedas. The deadly serious jousting was far from over, even to the extent that Nathaniel Pryor, the husband of Maria Teresa Sepulveda, filed a petition for 4000 acres of additional Dominguez land. Finally, in 1841 the Dominguez family officially transferred its rights to 32,000 acres of land to the Sepulvedas, leaving a residual Rancho San Pedro of 43,000 acres. It would be fair to say there was little love lost between the two families. Meanwhile, feuding was going on within each of the families over tenant-in-common holdings of rancho lands.

The tenant-in-common concept was the basic legal doctrine which held the Californio ranchos as entities despite the distribution of rancho interests to the numerous heirs of an estate. The Californios in the main had large families. When Don Bernardo Yorba died in 1858, he left more than twenty children, many of whom were married and all of whom had interests in the rancho. The tenant-in-common concept worked if there was a strong head of the family or a weaker man being protected by the orderly family traditions of the past. If there was neither, the splintered interests inevitably passed into the hands of individuals outside the family, which in turn was followed by partition suits of the outsiders to break up the rancho. With the stresses of the new American era and the large numbers of heirs, divisive forces within many of the rancho families became serious.

When the difficult times of the 1850s and 1860s arrived, the Dominguezes had a strong head of family; the Sepulvedas of Rancho Palos Verdes did not. Starting as a young man, Manual Dominguez had demonstrated an iron determination to hold together the family lands. When his brother, Jose Nasario, approached him in 1835 about buying Nasario's one-fifth interest in Rancho San Pedro, he did not hesitate. His brother's involvement in horse racing and gambling was well known on the South Coast, and it was equally clear that Nasario's tenant-in-common interest would inevitably pass out of the family's hands. Manuel accepted Nasario's offer of over 8000 acres of land for "thirty mares, each with colts, and a stallion . . . half of the colts male and the other half female of the Gutierrez stock."[7] Eventually, even Nasario realized he had sold his birthright for a pittance. But Manuel Dominguez was unyielding even in face of bitter charges by his brother of trickery and falsification. Nasario's claim was upheld at the District (Superior) Court in 1853, but the decision was reversed by the California Supreme Court the next year. Even so, Nasario took his claim to the Federal courts, where he again lost. The three years of litigation cost each of the brothers more than $5000 and ruined Nasario financially. Friends feared there would be personal violence between them. Passing on the street, the two brothers bitterly ignored each other.

Manuel Dominguez was not successful in acquiring the one-fifth interest of his younger brother when Pedro wanted to sell in the late 1840s. Nasario's bitterness was undoubtedly a factor, and Pedro's accumulation of liabilities was formidable. Pedro had little interest in the rancho and managed to stay heavily in debt while he and his wife, Maria Jesus Cota de Dominguez, lived in Los Angeles. When the news of the gold strikes in northern California reached the South Coast, Pedro could see a magical solution to all of his financial problems and become rich at the same time. This required borrowing more money to prospect for gold. John Temple, for many years a naturalized Californio, made him a loan in 1849. A few months later Pedro was back on the South Coast, having spent the money and being pressed for all his debts. With Manuel's advice in 1850, he made a decision. Pedro would deed nearly half of his one-fifth interest in Rancho San Pedro to Jose Antonio Aguirre, with the agreement that the Temple loan would be repaid. On the same day,

with his brother, Manuel Dominguez, as a witness, the remainder
of his inheritance was transferred to his wife. It was a half a
loaf and far better than none for holding the family lands. In
1852 Manuel bought 6900 acres from his older sister, Maria
Victoria, and the son of his younger sister, Maria Elena.

When Phineas Banning, heading a partnership including
John G. Downey, William Sanford and Benjamin D. Wilson, approached Dominguez about selling Rancho San Pedro lands in
what is now the Wilmington area, Manuel was hesitant. Banning
raised the price to $20,000 for 2400 acres, and Manuel agreed
finally to sell, in 1854. He could see the long-range potential of
the Wilmington lands as well as Banning. On the other hand, he
had the mounting costs of litigation with his brother and the
expenses of obtaining a land patent to the rancho. From the
time of the Wilmington tract sale until his death twenty-eight
years later, Manuel Dominguez managed to hold 28,000 acres
of Rancho San Pedro. His old antagonist, Jose Loreto Sepulveda,
was not so fortunate.

The final partition of Rancho Los Palos Verdes was made in
1882. Jose Loreto Sepulveda had been dead for more than a
year, and it made no difference anyway. As head of the family,
he had watched the Sepulvedas' holdings of 32,000 acres disappear into outside hands except for 3640 acres held by the
heirs of his brother Diego and fifty acres owned by his brother
Juan. It was a familiar story for most of the Californios—inter-
necine bitterness among the family tenants-in-common; a weak
head of the family; and the problems and expenses of proving
land patents before the United States Land Commission and the
Federal courts.

The three-man board of the United States Land Commission
began regular hearings in San Francisco early in 1852. Its charter
was to examine the validity of all California titles held under
Spanish or Mexican grants. The board met for five years, including a two-year extension. It heard approximately 800 cases
covering the title of 12,000,000 acres of land. Seven commissioners

served during the board's five-year life—a personnel turnover which certainly slowed up the board's work. The commission approved 520 claims and rejected 273. In nearly all of the cases the board's decisions were taken into the Federal courts either by the Government or by the claimant. The courts in the main sustained the decrees of the Board of Land Commissioners. On balance, the board carried out its assignments about as well as could be expected with the extent of technical complexities involved.

But to the Californios the Board of Land Commissioners meant endless time and expense along with all the problems of unfamiliarity with the American language and American judicial processes. A not insignificant burden to the South Coast was the fact that the land hearings were in San Francisco, hundreds of miles away. To the Californio " . . . The Land Law, preemption and occupancy rights, and the 'jungle-thickets' of land litigation made him not only violently angry but also mystified him."[8]

Not only were the Californios' titles being examined; they found that the American law on riparian or water rights was entirely different from that of their past experience. The owner of a large grant under Spanish or Mexican rule had very naturally chosen his land so as to have as large an amount of running water as possible. Available water for irrigation became attached to the grant. The Americans, on the other hand, applied the English common laws of riparian rights to California. This was the concept of compelling the user of water from a stream to turn back into the natural channel the water that had been used to turn his mill wheel. Such a legal doctrine was absurd when applied to a semi-arid country requiring irrigation. Gradually, the state legislature and the courts evolved a system of water laws adapted to the climate of California.

The Californios did have the state Trespass Act of 1850 which set rigid and expensive fencing requirements on settlers to keep out wandering stock. The law was not repealed until 1872, about the time barbed wire was becoming generally available. While it aided the ranchos financially, the Trespass Act became a source of real friction and hatred between the settlers and the large landowners. J. W. North, founder of the Riverside Colony, expressed the bitterness of the settler: " . . . It is a contest between advancing civilization and obsolete barbarism."[9]

As the sixties approached, the Californios on the South Coast were defending themselves on three fronts—the titles of their lands, their water rights and settler hatred and harassment. Further, they were in debt and the cattle boom had ended.

CHAPTER 5

"A man who couldn't drive a stage down that hill"

Passengers arriving by sea for Los Angeles in 1852 had the choice of riding a half-broken horse with a hard mouth for more than twenty miles from San Pedro, or taking Phineas Banning's stage line. Horace Bell, who arrived on the steamer *Sea Bird* from San Francisco with some twenty other passengers, decided on the latter:

> At San Pedro we found two stages of the old army ambulance variety to which were being harnessed a vicious-looking herd of bronco mules. . . . A sailor-looking fellow, who seemed to be at least half-seas-over sat on the driver's seat (in our stage) and held all the lines together in one hand. . . . Two savage-looking Mexicans stood with lassoes tightly drawn on the leading mules, while two others stood in a flanking position with the reatas ready to be used as whips to urge the animals forward. . . . A portly-looking man called Banning came around with a basket on his arm, and offered to each of the passengers an ominous-looking black bottle, remarking: "Gentlemen, there is no water between here and Los Angeles." . . . Banning then laughingly remarked that the drivers usually expected the passengers to bet something on the trip, "just enough to make it interesting." . . .[1]

Bell goes on to tell about the two stages jostling each other on the rutted and rocky trail, careening up and down stream beds and small arroyos, with the drivers, outriders and passengers liberally sampling the black bottles of aguardiente. The mules came up San Pedro Road in Los Angeles at a full gallop followed by a pack of nipping and yapping mongrel dogs which grew in number by the minute as the stages spun into First Street and finally pulled up with a flourish at the Bella Union Hotel on

Main Street. The trip cost young Bell fifty-five dollars in bets (his stage lost the race) and ten dollars in stage fare.

When J. L. Tomlinson set up a competitive line, the stage races were more feverish if possible and probably more honest. With the new competition the stage fares ranged from one to ten dollars, depending on what the traffic would bear.

Traveling in and out of the South Coast during the 1850s was a rugged experience and decidedly not cheap. Cabin passage from the open roadstead of San Pedro to San Francisco cost fifty-five dollars and took four days. Freight was as high as twenty-five dollars a ton. The small steamers, such as the *Sea Bird*, slammed into the prevailing seas moving into and down the coast and groped their way through the fog and dangerously fickle weather around Point Conception. If the passenger felt like eating (most did not), the fare was hard bread, salt beef, potatoes and black coffee with no sugar.

In 1858 John Butterfield started a semi-weekly stage under a government postal subsidy, from San Francisco to Memphis via Los Angeles, Fort Yuma, Tucson, El Paso and St. Louis. The fare from Los Angeles to Memphis was $150, with an initial schedule of twenty-four days, later reduced to twenty-one. The government subsidy for the Butterfield route was high—$600,000 a year—particularly when the second year's postal receipts were only $27,000. Not only were postal receipts low; so was passenger enthusiasm, considering the rigors of crossing the southern deserts and the fact that the stage traveled for hundreds of miles in Apache country. High-wheeled freight wagons, each carrying two and one-half tons of freight and hauled by a ten-mule team, followed the Butterfield route from Los Angeles as far as Fort Yuma.

The principal stage and wagon route to northern California was inland across the formidable Tehachapi Mountains to Fort Tejon, thence to White River, Visalia, Gilroy, San Jose and San Francisco. The Los Angeles-San Francisco stage fare was thirty dollars. The San Fernando Pass of the Santa Susana Mountains was the first major barrier on the route north. At one narrow gap "the road was so precipitous that the teamsters were some- times compelled to turn to the slow and difficult expedient, adopted by overland immigrant trains only as a last resort, of lowering or raising their wagons by means of ropes."[2]

After Phineas Banning had pioneered a route across the pass in 1855, he induced a group of South Coast citizens to contribute several thousand dollars to do some grading in the worst pass areas. However, it was many years before the main road to northern California was much more than a rutted and precipitous trail, with the inevitable washouts of the winter rains and the flash desert mountain floods of the summer months.

By 1851 the Mormon Trail from San Bernardino to Salt Lake City had been carefully surveyed by the first major Mormon ex- pedition to enter southern California. Mormon supply stations were then established en route. The present automobile road up the Cajon Pass, across the Mojave Desert to Las Vegas and then to Salt Lake City roughly follows the Mormon Trail. The stretch from San Bernardino to Las Vegas, including the Death Valley area, covers some of the most barren and desolate country in the world, interspersed with desert mountain ranges. Temperatures in the summer months can reach 130 degrees, and there is the strong likelihood of abrasive blowing sand and alkali dust at any time of year. Notwithstanding the rigors of the route, by the mid-fifties the Mormon Trail was being used routinely for freight, with charges of $400 to $500 a ton.

Much was expected from a communications viewpoint when a telegraph line was completed from San Francisco to Los Angeles in 1860. Phineas Banning of course had sold the idea that the new line should be extended to Wilmington. The lines worked only sporadically, even to the extent that shortly after the Wil- mington line was put into operation "there were many complaints that both poles and wire had fallen to the ground, blocking the thoroughfare and entangling animals in such a way to become a nuisance. Indeed, there was soon a public demand either to repair the telegraph or to remove it altogether and throw the equipment away."[3] Unfortunately, the line to San Francisco also worked only sporadically for years and received only limited use as a result. As late as 1867 it cost nine dollars to send a message of forty-four words between the two cities.

The gold prosperity of northern California brought clipper ships and steam vessels converging on San Francisco from all over the world. Along with mining and commercial enterprises, the range and valley lands of northern California began to fill with settlers. The southern cow counties soon realized that the state government would give little support to, and had no interest in, their roads and other public works requirements, and the local county boards of supervisors had no money. Los Angeles County in 1860 had a population of only 11,000 and covered an area of nearly 9000 square miles, nearly twice its present size. Further, there were strong feelings that sooner or later the large ranchos of southern California would be taxed out of existence by a state government controlled by the business interests of the northern part of the state.

Andres Pico introduced an 1859 joint resolution in the state assembly calling for the withdrawal of the counties of Los Angeles, San Diego, San Bernardino, Santa Barbara and San Luis Obispo from California, and the formation of the Territory of Colorado. Pico told the legislature that passage of the resolution was "the only salvation of our properties and happiness."[4] As it turned out, the northern part of California had little or no interest in whether the cow counties left California or not. Both houses of the state legislature readily approved Andres Pico's resolution, and the voters of the five counties concerned ratified it. However, with the onrushing events of the Civil War, the bill establishing the new territory died in the Congress. It would not be the last time, however, that serious proposals would be made for the two parts of California to go their separate ways.

With the hostile deserts and high mountains and no roads, the South Coast depended on sea transportation until the arrival of the railroads. Yet there were no harbors for hundreds of miles north of San Diego. San Pedro was a roadstead in a large open bay. Vessels arriving at San Pedro in the 1850s and 1860s undoubtedly shared some of Richard Henry Dana's feelings of some years before, after he rolled cargoes up the steep sixty-foot bluffs and carried hides over the kelp-covered rocks while his captain worried about southeast gales: "Two days brought us to San Pedro, and two days more to our own no small joy, gave us our last view of that place which was universally called the hell of California and seemed designed in every way for wear and tear on sailors."[5]

The Coast Survey Directory of 1858 cautioned vessels coming through the Santa Barbara Channel not to mistake the Palos Verdes peninsula for an island projected against the mountains to the south and eastward. It recommended anchoring about one mile inland of Point Fermin and a half mile from the San Pedro bluffs in line with Dead Man's Island, with an anchoring depth of three fathoms. In the winter months, vessels were advised to anchor further out and more to the southward of Dead Man's Island "in order to slip the cable and go to sea should a heavy southeaster spring up."[6] Considerably less than two acres in extent, Dead Man's Island consisted principally of a forty-foot-high eroded rock whose summit covered an area about fifty by one hundred feet. It was situated 3000 feet seaward from Rattlesnake (Terminal) Island in the present main channel of the harbor. The rock was not blasted out of the channel until 1928.

The Coast Survey Directory failed to mention that ship captains were also concerned about extremely strong northeast (santana) winds which began blowing from the desert with little or no warning "over flat country with a rake of more than a league of water."[7] The first recorded shipwreck in the San Pedro roadstead was the American brig *Danube*. The brig anchored far too close to Dead Man's Island and the bluffs, and a santana drove her onto the rocks of Point Fermin.

Passengers and freight were unloaded into lighters from the vessels standing in the roadstead. The lighters were brought across a bar with a depth of only eighteen inches of water at low tide, and came alongside a dock at Timm's Point or nearby Sepulveda Landing opposite Dead Man's Island, near present-day Twenty-second and Miner streets. August W. Timm had jumped ship in San Francisco early in the Gold Rush and then come to Los Angeles as an agent for several San Francisco shipping firms. After the *Mary Jane* went aground in a southeaster, Timm floated portions of the hull and deckhouse to a tiny promontory of land. The wreckage acted as a jetty, and the tides deposited sand and silt around it. Some years later the army transport *Abraham Lincoln* came ashore in another southeaster, and Timm expanded his jetty further. This with nearby Sepulveda Landing was the port of Los Angeles until Phineas Banning set up his own stage and freight terminal in 1858 at the back of the swampy estuary about five miles closer to Los Angeles by road.

J. L. Tomlinson's competition on stages and freight, combined with storms and surges which made for delays in unloading the lighters, finally persuaded Banning and his partner, David W. Alexander, to establish a new terminal. Several years earlier Banning had been able to raise the capital necessary to meet Manuel Dominguez's high price of $20,000 for 2400 acres of land in the estuary area. Banning called the development New San Pedro and then Wilmington after his birthplace in Delaware. Initially, using a small steam tug, the *Cricket,* the loaded lighters were maneuvered up the 100-foot-wide channel of the estuary with a water depth of six to ten feet at mean low tide for a distance of about two miles from Dead Man's Island. Opposite the new landing, the lighters were towed over a bar into what a few years later the San Diego *Union* referred to as "Banning's goose pond."

The new landing at Wilmington was opened by Phineas Banning with his usual pomp and circumstance, including decorated lighters and Los Angeles society women pretending to haul in lines. He gave a yachting party the next year which was the first of its kind on the South Coast. Fifty or sixty guests were invited, most of whom left at dawn from Los Angeles in Banning's stages. Arriving at Wilmington, they had breakfast. The

guests then boarded his new little tug *Comet,* which came alongside the U.S. Coast Survey ship *Active* standing off Dead Man's
Island. Two hours later they were at Catalina Island. Harris
Newmark, who was in the party and reported the event, did not
say whether the *Active* went to the Isthmus or Timm's Cove
(Avalon). At any event, after going ashore they left the Island
in the late afternoon and were back in Los Angeles by ten in the
evening. It was a long day—particularly making the trip twice
over a remarkably bad stage road between Los Angeles and
Wilmington.

Even by the mass-media standards of the 1970s, Phineas
Banning could qualify as having the maximum of color and
personality. He was a hard-driving extrovert with a facility for
making money and spending it with equal gusto. A big broad
man, he had the born athlete's timing and cold nerve to handle
beautifully a six-horse stage, an ability much admired in a land
of fine horsemen. Horace Bell described how Banning nearly
killed himself in the course of laying out a stage route across
the Santa Susana and Tehachapi Mountains in 1854:

> He had succeeded in reaching the summit of San Fernando,
> and the question among his nine wondering passengers who had
> toiled up the mountain on foot was how the stage would ever
> descend, all declaring it was an act of madness to attempt it.
> Banning laughingly assured them "it was all right; that a man
> who couldn't drive a stage safely down that hill was no driver
> at all, and should confine himself to ox-teaming in the valley."[8]

He took the stage over the precipice and down the slope,
sometimes the horses ahead of the stage, and sometimes the
stage ahead of the horses. The passengers found Banning, his
stage and his horses piled up in a thicket of chaparral at the
foot of the mountain. As Bell reported it, the passengers slid down
the mountain to salvage what they could. They found a bruised
and scratched Banning, who assured them: "Didn't I tell you so,
a beautiful descent, far less difficult than I anticipated. I intended

that staging to Fort Tejon and Kern River should be a success. Gentlemen, you see my judgment is good."[9] Some of what he said was true. A few months later, at his urging and that of Abel Stearns, enough money was raised by volunteer subscriptions to start grading the beginnings of a passable stage and freight trail to northern California.

Phineas Banning was twenty years of age when he arrived on the South Coast via Panama in 1851. He was hired by Douglas & Sanford, who were hauling freight and passengers to Los Angeles from San Pedro. Shortly thereafter he went to work for Temple & Alexander, buying out Temple's share and forming a new partnership with David W. Alexander. With the cattle boom in full swing, business was good, not only for his firm but for his competitors, Tomlinson, Timm and Diego Sepulveda. Banning had an idea which he finally sold to a reluctant Alexander, his new partner. Why not buy four large new Concord coaches, the standard of their day, to replace the uncomfortable and ramshackle stagecoaches that were being used? He brushed aside Alexander's response that such coaches would cost over a thousand dollars apiece. With a new customhouse and the cattle boom, he was convinced that the partnership could get the bulk of the passenger traffic; and he was right. The new coaches were a sensation. By 1854 the partnership had 500 mules, forty wagons and fifteen stages on the Los Angeles-San Pedro route. Banning began making the long run to Salt Lake City over the Mormon Trail and started freighting to Fort Yuma.

By the time Banning was in his late twenties he considered San Pedro his bailiwick, along with Fort Tejon and Fort Yuma. He was well on his way to becoming a very large transportation frog in a small pond. Certainly, the 1853 Fourth of July celebration which was put on by Banning and his partner along with their Californio friends showed a powerful and prosperous twenty-two-year-old man.

Some 2000 people gathered in San Pedro from scores of miles around, for a solid two days of barbecues, drinking, betting and feats of horsemanship, punctuated by appropriate oratory and miscellaneous brawling. Don Juan Sepulveda brought the very elderly cannon used by the Californios in the Rancho San Pedro skirmish with the American sailors and marines seven years before. The cannon was loaded on a lighter and taken to Dead Man's Island. Blocks and tackle were rigged, and the cannon was hauled to the top of the rock. With many liquid toasts to Californio-Americano friendship, the cannon was fired over the grave boards of the six Americans who had been killed or had died of wounds received in the action near Dominguez Hill.

It was quite a celebration at the desolate little port of San Pedro. Phineas Banning was in his element. Throughout his life he loved to give parties for business and pleasure. In his early years, with a booming laugh and dressed in shirt sleeves, red suspenders, heavy shoes and too short trousers, he was a conspicuous man. As he grew older, there was no question he liked titles—preferably military ones. It was natural he would become a general in the rather vaguely defined and mostly paper state militia established during the Civil War. He loved the title of "General" and was universally given it, albeit with a considerable degree of irony at times. Some of his close friends sporadically referred to him as "Admiral" because of his San Pedro activities. But whatever his personal foibles might be, Phineas Banning and the southern California frontier were made for each other.

CHAPTER 6

"In wickedness it was unlimited"

The Spanish colonizing mechanism had been well burnished in Mexico, and despite the long distances and tenuous communications, had worked well in Alta California. Backed by a strong militaristic and evangelistic tradition developed over hundreds of years, the presidio, pueblo and mission system quickly became strong and viable in the new province. Four presidios were established in Alta California at San Diego, Santa Barbara, Monterey and San Francisco. These were military strong points from which the mobile forces operated to protect the frontier and hold the mission Indian population in check. Three pueblos were founded—Los Angeles, Santa Cruz and San Jose. Each pueblo was established on about 17,000 acres of land. Civilian settlers of the pueblo were each given a building site with land for an orchard and a garden. The large remainder of the available land of the pueblo was used as a common pasture for stock, and the land title remained with the pueblo.

A chain of missions was established by Spain about a day's horseback ride apart extending from San Diego to San Francisco. Each mission was assigned but did not own an enormous tract of land. For example, the San Fernando mission properties covered nearly 350 square miles. The purpose of the missions under the Spanish colonization policy and operated by the Franciscans was threefold—to convert the Indians, to settle them on mission lands as loyal subjects to Spain and to provide them with food, clothing and shelter.

The final aspect of Spanish land policy in Alta California was the allocation of a limited number of land grants to private individuals. In most instances the lands were given to former soldiers of New Spain. Of the twenty-odd grants, most of the major ones were in southern California.

By the 1820s the frontier had been secured, and few of the sporadic Indian attacks or revolts took the Spanish by surprise. For better or worse, the missions accomplished their task. Indians were settled on mission lands by the thousands, but many died making the adjustment. Stock flourished. The San Gabriel mission alone had over 25,000 head of cattle with a large number of horses along with hogs and sheep. In the semi-arid southern California climate, systematic irrigation systems were developed by the missions, with orchards, vineyards and crops planted. As one of the pueblos, Los Angeles, with a thousand population, functioned as a military post and an orderly trading center for the South Coast.

With Mexican independence from Spain and the passage of land-reform acts by the new country, it was inevitable that sooner or later the Spanish colonizing system in Alta California would be sharply modified. Headed by Governor Manuel Micheltorena, a systematic campaign was launched by a group of Californios to have the land held by the missions returned to the public domain. The secularization of the missions and distribution of their lands and stock was finally made effective by decree in 1833 after five years of turmoil. The leaders of Mexico had more important things to concern them, and there was little interest in the remote province of Alta California, which had been established initially as a base for the Philippine galleons of Spain that no longer came to Acapulco. What vague government existed in Alta California was almost as bad as none at all. The numerous bloodless coups would have been comical except for the effect on the province. The missions, their people and their lands were ripe for the picking by the favorites of whomever was the current Mexican governor of Alta California. Systematic defense of the frontiers and policing of the settled areas disintegrated.

Stragglers and drifters, salted with a dribble of foreigners with highly questionable backgrounds, began to accumulate in

Los Angeles. Shortly thereafter came many of the displaced mission Indians, thrown out of a paternalistic and rigorous environment to which they had laboriously adapted over several generations. Los Angeles needed one more major ingredient to make it a witches' cauldron—the dregs of the American frontier. That was provided after the Gold Rush when vigilante committees in San Francisco ran the backwash of the gold mines out of the city. Los Angeles was the logical roosting place for a sordid assortment of murderers, thieves, badmen and outlaws who had heard about the cattle boom on the South Coast. By the 1850s the scruffy little town of 4000 people was having twenty to thirty murders a month, not including the periodic lynchings.

The Bella Union Hotel in Los Angeles advertised itself as "the best hotel south of San Francisco." Horace Bell, who previously had spent several years in the gold fields, viewed this claim with some cynicism in 1852:

> The house was a one-story flat-roofed adobe, with a corral in the rear, extending to Los Angeles Street, with the usual great Spanish portal. . . . On the north side of the Bella Union corral extending from the back door of the main building to Los Angeles Street, were numerous pigeon-holes, or dog-kennels. These were the rooms for the guests of the Bella Union. In rainy weather the primitive earthen floor was sometimes, and generally, rendered quite muddy by the percolation from the roof above, which in height from floor to ceiling, was about six or seven feet. The rooms were not over 6 x 9 in size. . . . The bar was well patronized. . . . The bartender wore an old dragoon coat and a red hat; a vicuna so common in the country at the time; open-legged Mexican calzoneros, with jingling buttons from hip to bottom, and by no means immaculate under-linen; protruding beneath his flowing robe could be seen the ugly looking Colt's revolver, while, with the fringe-work of his Mexican sash could be seen a chain of ponderous golden nuggets that hung from his fob. . . . In one corner beside the bar stood a double-barrelled shotgun, while, lying in convenient reach, could be seen a couple of Colts of the old army pattern, carrying half-ounce balls. . . . Some of the patrons who came and went from the Bella Union

bar were dressed in the gorgeous attire of the country, some half ranchero, half miner; others were dressed in the most modern style of tailorship; all, however, had slung to their rear the never-failing pair of Colts, generally with the accompaniment of the bowie knife.[1]

Other travelers also commented on the fleas and the resonant snoring of fellow guests at the hotel. The Bella Union's bar and its exceedingly well armed patrons could be duplicated at other respectable saloons and gambling houses, such as the Montgomery, the Palace and the El Dorado, as well as the drinking dives and vice dens in the town.

The most widely known street in Los Angeles for a generation after American rule was the Calle de Los Negros. Probably named for early Sonoran settlers of dark complexion and called Nigger Alley by the Americans, it was a short street extending from the upper end of Arcadia to the Plaza. As James M. Guinn described it:

> In length it did not exceed five hundred feet, but in wickedness it was unlimited. On either side it was lined with saloons, gambling halls, dance houses and disreputable dives. It was a cosmopolitan street. Representatives of different races and many nations frequented it. Here the ignoble red man, crazed with aguardiente, fought his battles, the swarthy Sonoran plied his stealthy dagger, and the click of a revolver mingled with the clink of gold at the gaming table when some chivalric American felt that his word of "honah" had been impugned. The Calle de Los Negros in the early '50s, when the deaths from violence averaged one a day, was the central point from which the wickedness radiated.[2]

Guinn could have expanded his comment on the Indians, as their activities provided a major weekly fillip to Calle de Los Negros and the nearby areas. By the 1850s the vineyard and other employers immediately around Los Angeles began paying off their Indian labor in raw aguardiente on each Saturday evening. Saturday night was drunkenness and debauchery; the next day was worse: "By four o'clock on Sunday afternoon, Los Angeles Street from Commercial to Calle de Los Negros, Aliso

Street from Los Angeles to Alameda, and Calle de Los Negros,
would be crowded with a mass of drunken Indians, yelling and
fighting. Men and women, boys and girls, tooth and toe nail,
sometimes and frequently with knives, but always in a manner
that would strike the beholder with horror."[3] At sundown, the
Indians were driven to a corral by the town marshal. They were
held there until Monday morning, when their bail was paid by
the vineyard and other employers on an auction basis, and the
weekly cycle began again.

Violent and organized crime reached a crescendo during the
1850s and 1860s on the South Coast, with Los Angeles being
the festering crime center. The Manilas raid on San Juan Capistrano was typical of the emerging pattern of organized terrorism.
As late as 1865, San Bernardino believed that it would be under
systematic outlaw attack. There were solid grounds supporting
the intelligence that a large outlaw band was planning to come
down Cajon Pass from the upper desert, take the town and sack
it. The raid did not take place, but whether the planning of
such an operation was fantasy or fact, it could have occurred.
Robbery and murder on the roads and trails to Los Angeles
became increasingly frequent. The Los Angeles *Star's* report of
November 29, 1862, dealing with John Rains' murder while coming from Rancho Azusa to Los Angeles, was an indication of the
times:

> . . . Yesterday the body of Mr. Rains was discovered. It was
> lying about four hundred yards from the main road in a cactus
> patch. The body gave evidence that the unfortunate gentleman
> had been lassoed, dragged from his wagon by the right arm
> which was torn from the socket, and the flesh mangled from
> the elbow to the wrist; he had been shot twice in the back, also
> in the left breast and right side . . The body was not far from
> where the wagon had been concealed. . . . The funeral will take
> place tomorrow evening from the Bella Union Hotel. . . .[4]

A Manuel Cerradel was convicted for the Rains murder and
received a ten years' prison sentence. While he was being taken
by tug to a ship in the San Pedro roadstead for transport to San
Quentin, a group of vigilantes hanged him from the mast.

Phineas Banning's reaction to the death of his brother-in-law a year later was predictable. John Sanford was murdered on the trail from Fort Tejon to Los Angeles by Charles Wilkins, a well-known Calle de Los Negros character. Wilkins was run down by a posse and brought to Los Angeles for trial. Banning stalked into the courtroom, drew a pistol and was forcibly restrained at the last moment from killing Wilkins. Shortly thereafter, Banning led a vigilante group which broke into the jail, took Wilkins to the Tomlinson & Griffith corral and lynched him.

The police and the courts were not remotely organized or staffed to handle the wave of violence which spewed over the South Coast after the Gold Rush. Superficially, the Los Angeles jail in 1852 would appear to have been a strong crime deterrent, if one was unfortunate enough to be incarcerated there. The jail was in an old adobe house west and up the hill from the Bella Union Hotel. A long and large pine log had been dragged into the sala of the house. Heavy staples were driven into the log at four-foot intervals. Each prisoner was shackled at the feet with iron chains, and a center chain about a foot long was attached to the staple in the log. Presumably with maneuvering, there was room enough for the prisoner to stretch out on his back. The new jail built a year or so later was somewhat better in its facilities; at least the log was eliminated.

The atrocious and primitive jail facilities represented only a symptom of the underlying lack of law and order. The California governmental system had been disintegrating for years under the chaotic Mexican rule, and the flimsy law apparatus of the new American state for the remote southern cow counties was as bad. With no funds and disorganized public support the result at times was near anarchy on the South Coast and in Los Angeles. The vigilantes and their lynching bees were sure to appear with the strong support of the people.

In one year (1854) there were twenty-two hangings in Los Angeles. Most of them were without the law. The vigilantes had a penchant for lynching at the gateway of the Tomlinson & Griffith corral on Temple Street between Buena Vista and New High Streets or on improvised gallows on Fort Hill. However, they

were catholic in their location selection, depending on the mood
and timing. In one instance, according to Harris Newmark, a
lynching was reported in advance of the fact:

> The lynching-bee seemed likely to come off about three
> o'clock in the afternoon, while the steamer for San Francisco
> was to leave at ten o'clock on the same morning; so that the
> schedules did not agree. . . . Billy Workman planned to print
> a full account of the execution in time to reach the steamer. So
> Billy sat down and wrote out every detail, even to the con-
> fession of the murderer on the improvised gallows; and several
> hours before the tragic event actually took place, the wet news-
> sheet was aboard the vessel and on its way north A few surplus
> copies gave the lynchers the unique opportunity, while watching
> the stringing up, of comparing the written story with the affair
> as it actually occurred.[5]

The citizen groups who both literally and figuratively took
the law into their own hands were ill-organized and often had a
strong mob flavor. At the best, the widely accepted vigilante
practices of the times were a palliative until the basic frontier
conditions changed in the 1870s. More effective was the establishment of a volunteer mounted police unit, called the Rangers,
in Los Angeles. The unit had about a hundred names on its
rolls. Horses and money were provided by men such as Don Pio
Pico, Phineas Banning, Don Ygnacio Del Valle, John Rowland
and Isaac Williams. Similar Ranger groups were organized in
El Monte and San Bernardino. The Rangers worked in conjunc-
tion with the Californios on the ranchos, the sheriff and the
military garrisons on the South Coast and Fort Yuma. Ranger
posses were sent throughout southern California over the years,
and undoubtedly helped to slow somewhat the rise of crime.

The better side of Los Angeles lived cheek by jowl with the
crime, violence and lynchings during the 1850s. Hard liquor was
consumed in quantity both inside and outside of the numerous
bars and saloons. Yet some of the young men of the town would
put on small dances with only lemonade being served when the

girls arrived with their dueñas. The orchestra might consist of a guitar, a harp and perhaps a flute. Serenading was also in favor. The men with their dates and dueñas would go in a group to a popular girl's house, where they would sing and be invited in for cake and wine.

The numerous religious festivals were celebrated with processions, fireworks and bonfires. The annual Corpus Christi festival was the most elaborate. It started and ended at the church across from the Plaza, and the area, which needed it, had been thoroughly cleaned for the occasion. Californio families erected temporary altars in front of their town houses, the altars being decorated with costly materials and even jewelry. A procession started from the church, with the participants dressed in white and carrying lighted candles, banners and flowers. It wound around the Plaza and the neighboring streets, stopping at each of the altars in front of the town houses and returning to the church several hours later. Even the Calle de Los Negros was quiet. On Christmas Eve, a group of players and singers (Los Pastores) left Rancho Los Feliz, stopping at each of the major Californio houses in Los Angeles while singing Christmas songs and giving a short miracle play. For a few days after Christmas, the play and the singing was repeated at the neighboring ranchos. All of this was part of the old ways and traditions, symbolized best perhaps by one man, the patriarch of the Lugo family.

Heads turned and many hats came off when Don Antonio Maria Lugo rode up Los Angeles' Main Street in the 1850s. He would geet his friends with "estimado" or "amado compadre" as his horse wove through the traffic to his town house beyond First Street on San Pedro Road. Lugo, then in his seventies, was "tall, straight and supple with a splendid military carriage"[8] and known among the Californios as a horseman of great style to be imitated—"el cuerpo de Lugo." Even the Americans agreed that he was a sight to see, the elderly gentleman riding a responsive and beautiful horse, his ornamental sword strapped in Spanish-soldier fashion to a saddle heavy in silver. Don Antonio, like other rich Californios, wore pantaloons open at the side below the knee while riding or breeches of velvet or satin cloth when not, shoes of deerskin embroidered with gold and silver, an open-neck shirt of silk or velvet, and a short figured jacket. A sash was bound around his waist. The dark hat was stiff and broad-brimmed, lined with silk with a silver or gold cord encircling the crown. A dark-blue serape of broadcloth with velvet trimmings and thrown over the shoulder completed his dress.

Antonio Maria Lugo had been a Spanish soldier, then had settled in southern California some years after the founding of the missions. In 1810 he had received one of the few Spanish grants. Rancho San Antonio, comprising 30,000 acres and probably the most famous of the original grants, adjoined the public lands of Los Angeles on the southeast. The San Antonio grant was only part of Lugo's interests, which extended through California and into Sonora. As the most prestigious Californio during most of his long life span, he was expected to, and did, serve for years both as a Judge of the Plains and as the leader of the Californios in Los Angeles and the South Coast. The Lugo family by blood or marriage included such noted names as the Vallejos and the Wolfskills. He represented the Californios at their best in honor, courtesy, hospitality and horsemanship. Don Antonio died in 1860. His life and activities had spanned nearly the entire Californio era.

CHAPTER 7

"No filth shall be thrown in the zanjas"

"No filth shall be thrown in the zanjas (open ditches) carrying water for common use, nor into the streets of the city, nor shall any cattle be slaughtered in same."[1] This excellent 1850 ordinance of the first Common Council of Los Angeles was, of course, completely ignored by the town's inhabitants. Little attempt was made to collect "all the heads and remains of dead animals . . . that they might be set on fire and thoroughly consumed and purified."[2] It was the height of wishful thinking by the Common Council to believe that every citizen was going "to sweep in front of his habitation on Saturdays, as far as the middle of the street, or at least eight varas."[3]

Contributing to the debris were bodies of dead dogs shot down from the yapping and biting mongrel packs which exuberantly followed the horsemen, stages, wagons and carretas. In addition to providing domestic water the open water zanjas were used to wash dirty clothes and dispose of miscellaneous wastes. Sewers were nonexistent and outhouses the rule. It could be said without equivocation that the dirt streets of Los Angeles in the 1850s were filthy, smelly and dusty during the hot summer months. During the rainy months the clinging clay mud would be six inches to two feet deep. There were no sidewalks. What trees there had been in the town long since had been cut down for firewood, the only fuel.

Drinking water came from the zanjas or from water-cart peddlers. The town had built a small dam on the Los Angeles River as a collection point. A water wheel behind the dam raised the water to the main, or madre, zanja, which fed into a new brick reservoir in the Plaza. The dam in the river would periodically be swept away during the winter floods. Until it was re-built, the only water was from the cart peddlers.

Typhoid, surprisingly enough, was a recurring but not a major problem, nor was dysentery widely reported, except by new-comers. Rats were common but not as prevalent as in San Fran-cisco. Fleas were another matter; in abundance and activity travelers rated Los Angeles fleas second to none.

A number of doctors came to the South Coast during the 1850s and 1860s. Some were able and devoted men; some were neither. They came for adventure, for health or because of pasts they wanted to forget. Their out-of-town practice was initially handled on horseback, with their instruments and a large assort-ment of pills in the saddlebags. Later on they used light spring wagons or buggies with tops. In addition to fractures, gunshot wounds and knifing wounds, they saw diphtheria, tetanus, small-pox and typhoid. Major operations other than amputations were seldom attempted and then only under the direst necessity. Un-derstanding of the germ theory of disease and antiseptic prac-tices was still many years away. A doctor performing surgery prided himself on his speed. When tying blood vessels, he might hold the scalpel between his teeth. The lapel of his coat was often used to hold the threaded needles for sewing up the wound.

The state of the medical art in Los Angeles was probably no better or worse than in other isolated rural areas in the United States at the time. The family home medical chest usually in-cluded castor oil, ipecac and calomel, among other things. The children on the South Coast died as they did before and years after of the dreaded diphtheria, whooping cough and scarlet fever.

As early as 1850, four doctors formed the Los Angeles Medi-cal Faculty, with a standard schedule of fees. In the cattle-boom years and with very few doctors, the fee schedule was five dollars for an office visit, ten dollars for a night call, five dollars for each league (about three miles) traveled on a visit to the plains, five dollars for bleeding and ten dollars for cutting. These high fees were short-lived because of the collapse of the boom.

As a major sign of progress, Los Angeles finally had a resident dentist in the late 1850s. At about the same time, the Sisters of Charity founded the first hospital in the town, calling it the Los Angeles Infirmary. Initially it was in a house north of the Plaza which had been long occupied by Don Jose Maria Aguilar. The next year the Sisters bought adjacent land from Don Luis Arenas and subsequently built a two-story brick building.

The first major commercial building in Los Angeles was the Arcadia Block. It represented early physical evidence of the town's gradual transition from a Mexican pueblo. Abel Stearns built the two-story brick structure at the corner of Arcadia and Los Angeles streets, adjacent to his home, and named it after his wife. The first floor was well above the level of the street as a protection against flooding by the Los Angeles River. The building had iron doors and window shutters. Fabrication of these doors and shutters required Stearns to establish a foundry, the first industrial plant on the South Coast.

Shortly after the completion of the Arcadia Block in 1858, John Temple finished the south portion of the two-story Temple Block at the junction of Spring and Main streets. To the amazement of the Californios, Temple actually planted trees around the new structure and put in a sidewalk, the first in Los Angeles, consisting of bricks coated with roofing tar and a thin top layer of sand.

Temple also built a two-story brick building the next year to serve as the town market. The structure occupied a small block between Main and Spring streets just south of his first new building. Other than a town clock which worked only sporadically, a major item of interest to the citizens was the first theater/large meeting room on the second floor. After John Temple's death in 1866 the building was used as the county courthouse for many years.

It was just as well that commercial brick building construction did not start in Los Angeles until 1858. With no vertical reinforcing rods, the brick walls could have collapsed and the roofs fallen in during the two earthquakes which occurred during the previous several years.

The South Coast's history showed a long record of earthquakes, as Don Gaspar de Portola's expedition learned in 1769 when it was camped on the banks of the Santa Ana River. There were four violent earth shocks over a period of three hours. On December 8, 1812, when more than a hundred people were in attendance at Mass in the new stone church of Mission San Juan Capistrano, there were two massive shocks close together. The domes above the nave split open and fell on the people below. The high tower of the church swayed from north to south and then fell into the open courtyard. The other mission buildings stood the shocks but with heavy damage. Thirty-nine people were killed, and a great many more were injured. On the logarithmic Richter scale, this 1812 quake was between Magnitude 7 and 8, with the epicenter off the coast. While only a time coincidence, the greatest earthquake in recorded United States history occurred the same year in the Mississippi Valley below St. Louis. Reports at the time said the Mississippi River for a period actually reversed its flow.

Newcomers to the Los Angeles area after the Gold Rush received a major introduction to the South Coast's earthquake propensity during the evening of July 11, 1855. The quake was about Magnitude 6 on the Richter scale. (The Los Angeles earthquake of February 9, 1971, with an epicenter somewhat north of the San Fernando Valley, was 6.5 on the same scale.) The epicenter of the 1855 earth shocks was in the area between the San Gabriel and Los Angeles rivers and ". . . almost every structure in Los Angeles was damaged, and some of the walls were left with large cracks. Near San Gabriel, the adobe in which Hugo Reid's Indian wife dwelt was wrecked, notwithstanding that it had walls four feet thick with great beams of lumber. . . . In certain spots the ground rose; in others it fell; and with the rising and falling, down came chimneys . . . and even parts of roofs, while water in barrels, and also in several of the zanjas, bubbled and splashed and overflowed."[4] Aftershocks continued for months.

The populated areas of the South Coast were fortunate on the morning of January 9, 1857. A great earthquake of more than Magnitude 8 occurred on the San Andreas Fault, with its epicenter in the Tehachapi Mountains. The first shock was relatively light, but the succeeding ones grew rapidly in strength for nearly a three-minute period. In Los Angeles about a hundred miles away the population rushed into the streets and "horses and cattle broke loose in wild alarm."[5] Fortunately the damage in the town was no worse than in 1855. It was another matter in the Fort Tejon area of the Tehachapis: "Great rents were opened in the earth and then closed again, piling up a heap or dune of finely-powdered stone and dirt. Large trees were uprooted and hurled down the hillsides; and tumbling after them went the cattle."[6] While the adobe buildings at Fort Tejon were nearly leveled, no lives were lost at the fort.

The last great earthquake of the nineteenth century in California occurred along the Owens Valley Fault on March 26, 1872. It was Magnitude 8 or more on the Richter scale. In Los Angeles 200 miles away the force was strong enough to throw people out of bed. It was two days before the town heard of the tremendous violence of the quake in the Owens Valley and the resulting devastation there.

Relatively few of the population of Los Angeles could read with any facility in the 1850s. This was scarcely surprising, as the first school was not built until 1854, with instruction starting the next year. It was a two-story building located out in the country at Second and Spring streets, and it cost about $6000 to build. Fifteen years later, this school building was still considered too far away from the business center to hold a teachers' institute. Even by 1860 only about one-fifth of the town's children of grammar-school age were enrolled in school. The same year the state appropriated $2500 for the support of schools in Los Angeles County, basing the amount on school attendance. The northern mountain counties of El Dorado and Nevada received about the same amount. By the end of the Civil War, there were less than 600 pupils enrolled in sixteen schools in Los Angeles County, which included present-day Orange County. The average pay for the sixteen teachers for that year was $577.

Other than the first public school there were few buildings south of Second Street or on the low hills to the west of Main Street in the 1850s. The route south to the seaport was out San Pedro Road. The road east to San Gabriel, El Monte and San Bernardino was down Aliso Street to the Los Angeles River, which was forded generally just above where the main zanja tied into the dam at the river. The trail north to the San Joaquin Valley was up Sixth Street. The activities of the town were in the few blocks surrounding the Plaza. The two hotels, Bella Union and Lafayette, faced each other north of Commercial and the junction of Main and Spring streets. The town houses of the Californios were around the Plaza and in Sonoratown northwest of the Plaza in the general area of Eternity (North Broadway) and Virgin (Alpine) streets. A number of Sonorans had come from Mexico over the years and settled in single-story adobe row houses for living and operating small shops. Sonoratown had expanded in the 1850s with the influx of Mexicans who had tried their luck as miners in the gold fields and then drifted back southward to Los Angeles. The area was a closely knit community within a small town, retaining its own provincial customs, dialect and identity for many years.

It was appropriate that the Plaza de Toros would be in Sonoratown on Calle del Toros (Castellar Street). Bullfights in Los Angeles were fifth-rate by Mexican and Spanish standards. The bull ring consisted of a brightly painted staked corral, with a structure resembling a grandstand outside the ring enclosure. Announcements of a bullfight usually proclaimed that the toreador and his troop were fresh from triumphs in Mexico or Spain, but in fact they were Sonorans who worked at less glamorous tasks in town during the week. At times the bull made it uncomfortable for his amateur tormentors and broke through the ring enclosure, scattering the spectators until he was lassoed by a vaquero. Another popular sport at the Plaza de Toros was bear/bull fights. Even if the bear won, it was always killed. The

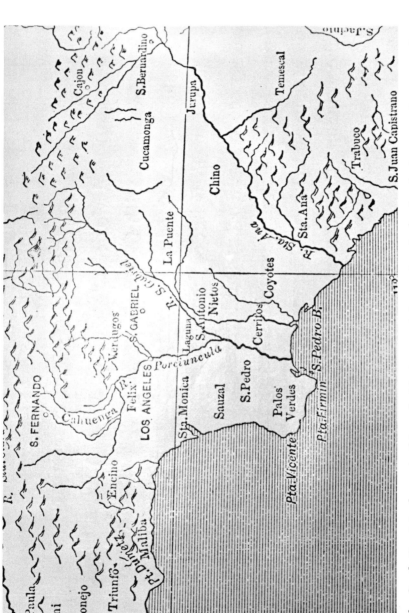

The South Coast is shown in this early Mexican period map that shows also the location of many ranchos of the Californios. From Bancroft, *courtesy of Title Insurance and Trust Company.*

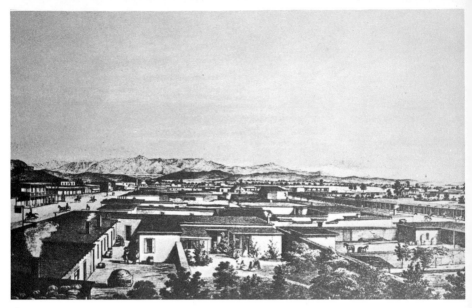

This 1857 drawing of Los Angeles gives the impression of neatness and orderliness in the small town. The facts were exactly the opposite. Lithograph by Kuchel & Dresel, *courtesy of Title Insurance and Trust Company.*

It was necessary to drive through the surf at one point north of San Buenaventura on the coastal trail to northern California. *Courtesy of Title Insurance and Trust Company.*

Abel Stearns. For nearly three decades he was the most wealthy and prominent of the Californios. *Courtesy of Security Pacific National Bank.*

Andres Pico. A longtime Californio leader, he hunted down the Flores-Daniel gang and introduced a resolution calling for southern California to become a separate territory. *Courtesy of Security Pacific National Bank.*

The interior of a Concord stagecoach shows the broad leather strap which kept passengers from being thrown from their seats on the rutted trails. *Courtesy of Wells Fargo Museum.*

Jose Andres Sepulveda. Owner of Rancho San Joaquin, he symbolized the strengths and weaknesses of the Californios during the 1850s and 1860s. From Henri Penelon, *courtesy of Charles W. Bowers Memorial Museum.*

Mission San Juan Capistrano before the church tower was toppled into the courtyard during the 1812 earthquake. The roof of the church fell into the nave, killing 39 persons. *Courtesy of Title Insurance and Trust Company.*

This fortunate mission Indian continued to work as a silversmith at Mission San Fernando. The lot of many Indians after the breakup of the missions was tragic. *Courtesy of Title Insurance and Trust Company.*

The two-wheeled carreta drawn by two oxen was the only vehicle used by the Californios until well into the American period. *Courtesy of Security Pacific National Bank.*

Calle de Los Negros, the infamous center of Los Angeles' gambling and vice, was the street next to the old Coronel adobe seen in the background of the photograph. *Courtesy of Los Angeles County Museum.*

Manuel Dominguez. In contrast to most of the Californios, he fought successfully to keep the bulk of his lands intact. *Courtesy of the Dominguez Estate.*

Juan Bandini. He welcomed American rule but then became embittered with the rancho-title investigations of the Land Commission. *Courtesy of Security Pacific National Bank.*

Lynchings in Los Angeles were common events at the peak of its frontier violence. This photograph may be of the hanging of Michael Lachenais in 1870. *Courtesy of Security Pacific National Bank.*

The Wilmington dock was built in 1858 by Phineas Banning. Steam tugs towed loaded lighters three miles from ships anchored in San Pedro roadstead. *Courtesy of Security Pacific National Bank.*

Water was lifted 36 feet by this wheel, which was part of the 1868 water-distribution system of Los Angeles. *Courtesy of Title Insurance and Trust Company.*

The first part of the Temple Block and the courthouse, which had a clock that worked only sporadically, were built by John Temple in the late 1850s. *Courtesy of Los Angeles County Museum.*

Harris and Sarah New-
mark. Their Los An-
geles marriage took
place in 1858. New-
mark became a wealthy
commodity merchant
and wrote a well-known
South Coast history.
From *Sixty Years in
Southern Calif.*, 2nd ed.

Advertising itself as "the best hotel south of San Francisco" in the 1850s, the Bella Union had tiny flea-ridden rooms and a large well-patronized bar. *Courtesy of Title Insurance and Trust Company.*

During the Civil War, camel expresses ran from Drum Barracks in Wilmington to Tucson and Fort Mojave. More than $1,000,000 was spent on construction of the Wilmington facility. *Courtesy of Title Insurance and Trust Company.*

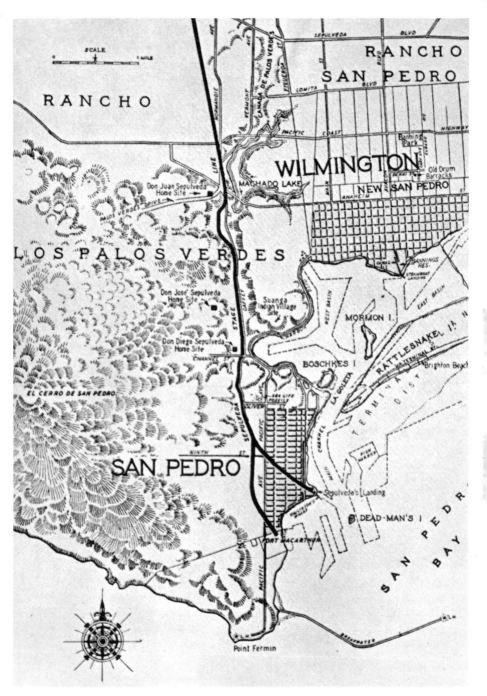

This 1925 map of San Pedro Harbor shows the original location of Dead Man's Island, as well as the estuary and Phineas Banning's dock at Wilmington. *Courtesy of Title Insurance and Trust Company.*

Phineas Banning. A l a r g e transportation frog in a small pond, he had a facility for making money and spending it with gusto. *Courtesy of Security Pacific National Bank.*

John G. Downey. Governor of California at 32, he was one of the breed of bright young men who arrived on the South Coast in the early 1850s. *Courtesy of Security Pacific National Bank.*

Californios did not like bears. In a rare burst of civic progressiveness, all bull and bull/bear fights were banned by Common
Council ordinance in 1860.

The patron of cockfights and a great many other things in
Sonoratown, and Los Angeles for that matter, was Mariano G.
Santa Cruz, who ran a grocery store and was a man who accumulated power among his people. The grave diggers at Campo
Santo, the Catholic cemetery north on Eternity Street, knew him
with respect. So did Tiburcio Vasquez, the famous bandido, a
few years later. Cockfights meant betting to Santa Cruz, and the
Californios liked to bet. The fights took place in Sonoratown and
occasionally in San Gabriel. A sport of the Californios in which
Mariano Santa Cruz could see only limited opportunities for
gain was the Correr el Gallo ("To Run the Rooster"). The concept of this sport was simple. A live rooster was buried in the
ground with its well-greased neck and head protruding. Each
rider in the competition would gallop over a course, bending
from the saddle to seize the greased neck of the rooster, and
return to the starting mark hopefully with the live bird. Still
another competition which the young men liked in the Spanish
tradition was galloping with a long spear at a suspended collection of small rings. The winner was the one with the greatest
number of rings on his lance.

Los Angeles was becoming bilingual during the 1850s, although Spanish remained the primary language. The weekly
Los Angeles *Star*, started in 1851 by John A. Lewis and John
McElroy, was printed half in Spanish, half in English for the few
hundred Americans. It was primarily an advertising medium,
as there was no telegraphic communication with the outside
world and the local news had already been covered by town
gossip. The *Star* got some competition in 1854 when C. N.
Richards and Company started the *Southern Californian*, a four-
page weekly later owned by Andres Pico. It also was published
in Spanish and English. Francisco P. Ramirez, a twenty-year-old
Californio who had worked for the *Star*, founded the weekly *El
Clamor Publico* in 1855, an all-Spanish-language newspaper
which he hoped would appeal to the Californios and the French

colony of several hundred people. For a time it was a popular sheet airing a blend of opinion and news which mirrored the views of the Californios. However, subscribers began to drop off, and it ceased publication in 1859.

Commerce in the town reflected the practices of a small and sleepy regional trading center. Stores stayed open until eight in the evening, with a siesta close-down in the early afternoon. The squeaking of the wooden wheels of a carreta coming into town was enough to bring the shopkeepers to their doors, for this hopefully was the signal of a buying expedition from a rancho. There were no hitching posts in front of the commercial shops, and very few in town. When a rider went into a shop, he attached a reata around the neck of his saddled horse and held the other end while in the shop. A pedestrian either walked around the kicking end of the horse, vaulted over the reata or jerked on the rawhide rope for the rider in the shop to lower it. The shops as well as the homes were lighted with tallow candles or rectified turpentine oil. Use of kerosene was some years away.

One of the business entrepreneurs of the town was Peter Biggs. He ran a business; he had an original turn of mind; and the ladies liked him. Horace Bell asserted that for a short time Biggs achieved a monopoly on the export of cats to San Francisco to catch rats until his love of gambling caught up with him. Peter Biggs was one of the first Negroes in Los Angeles, a freed slave who had served as a batman to an army officer. Biggs set himself up as a barber and wig-seller near the Bella Union Hotel in 1852, advertising his services and wares in the *Star*. He charged seventy-five cents for a haircut and fifty cents for a shave during the boom times. In his extracurricular activities he was rated a superior man about town and served as master of ceremonies at balls. During the Civil War, Biggs was a loud and firm supporter of the South. At one point he was picked up by a Federal patrol and dumped into the Drum Barracks' stockade at Wilmington. This did not dampen his enthusiasm or war opinions, and eventually his numerous friends got him released.

It seemed grossly unfair to the Los Angeles businessmen that all the gold discoveries appeared to be in northern California, with San Francisco and Sacramento receiving all the benefits. Obviously, the way to cure this regrettable situation was to encourage and sponsor gold prospecting throughout all of southern California and hope for the magic lode. Gold had been discovered near Newhall in 1842, ahead of the Sutter discovery. As the years passed, prospecting continued through the Tehachapis, the Owens River area, the San Gabriel and San Bernardino Mountains, and on to the Colorado River. Even Catalina Island had a short-lived boom. Gold was found in most of these places, but transportation, labor and supply costs were far too high in relation to the amount of gold to make it worthwhile. However, the prospecting and the limited mining operations did account for a fair part of Los Angeles' business activity in providing provisioning and wagons. By 1859 Goller & Baldwin were operating seven blacksmith forges, employing thirty men and carrying parts for fifty large freight wagons.

The total municipal budget for Los Angeles in 1859 was $15,000. The Common Council found it extremely difficult to raise money from taxation to supply even the most elementary services. As a painless way of raising some of the funds, it turned to the sale of public lands. As a former pueblo under the Spanish colonizing system, the public lands of Los Angeles still amounted to nearly 17,000 acres in 1856. As time passed, the lands were sold on a lot or acreage basis or given in payment for services to the municipality. O. W. Childs contracted to build a zanja and took land in payment in lieu of $1600. The Childs tract ran from present-day Sixth to Twelfth streets and Main to Figueroa streets. Dr. John S. Griffin bought 2000 acres of what is now the East Los Angeles area for fifty cents an acre, and he did not consider it any particular bargain, because it had limited water. One twenty-acre parcel west of town in the present Wilshire district was auctioned off for $150. By the early 1900s all that the city owned of the original 17,000 acres was a small amount of river-bottom land, some public building parcels and a few parks.

A substantial part of the town was planted to vineyards and some citrus, a carry-over of the mission tradition, but the citrus fruit was indifferent. The mission grape, on the other hand, was purple-black, medium-sized and thin-skinned. It was sweet and juicy. After the Gold Rush the mission grapes were sent in quantity by ship to San Francisco, packed in sawdust. As late as 1857 more than a million pounds were shipped north. At the height of the gold boom in San Francisco, the mission grapes retailed at twenty cents a pound; then, as vineyards were planted near San Francisco, the table-grape trade from the South Coast died out. Concurrently, however, wine production was increasing to the extent that by 1866 Los Angeles county was producing 600,000 gallons of wine and 70,000 gallons of aguardiente, due in substantial part to the vineyards of the Anaheim Colony coming on stream. There was plenty of aguardiente available to pay off the Indian laborers of the vineyards.

In contrast to the Anaheim Colony and San Bernardino, El Monte, or the Monte as it was called, seemed part of Los Angeles even though it was eleven or twelve miles away. The Monte boys were always willing to come to Los Angeles for a party, to form a posse or to participate in a lynching bee. The town of El Monte was founded on the banks of the San Gabriel River in 1851 by a group of immigrants from the Texan frontier. The land was rich and the community prospered. The settlers were known for their strong views, which ranged from states' rights to the right kind of hard liquor. The Monte boys worked hard and played hard. The *Star* reported one of their parties very well in 1855: "The Christmas cotillion party at the Monte, we learn was well attended by the elite of the thriving locality, and the dancing, feasting and gymnastic exercises continued until morning."[7]

CHAPTER 8

"The antithesis of Los Angeles"

The Mormons played a significant role in southern California during the 1850s. If Brigham Young's grand plan could have been carried out, the role would have been much more so.

The first elements of the great Mormon trek from Missouri reached present-day Utah in 1847. Three years later there were 20,000 Mormons in the area. They were bound together by a religion which was calculated on one hand to invite harassment from the gentiles, and on the other, to insure absolute obedience to the head of the church, Brigham Young. The Mormons were competent farmers and craftsmen working as a close-knit group under the rigid discipline imposed by a brilliant leader. Filled with religious zeal, missionary teams were at work in England and on the Continent for recruits to the Mormon faith. Many of the foreign converts came to Zion in Utah.

Brigham Young was strongly opposed to Utah remaining a territory, as this would continue to place it under gentile officials appointed by the Federal Government. Instead he wanted to found the state of Deseret, a Mormon state with the political independence guaranteed by the Federal Constitution. As part of his master plan, he needed a sea-water port, preferably a natural harbor. San Diego met the requirements as a port of entry for the English and European converts and for the import and export of Mormon commodities. He visualized a route to be Mormon-controlled from southern California across the deserts and mountains to Salt Lake City. It would be used for the movement of the new converts to Utah and trade with the Californios and the outside world.

Such a plan would require a major staging site in southern California near the Mojave Desert and which might become another Salt Lake City at the end of the long Mormon corridor. An expedition left Salt Lake City in 1851 to survey a route for way-stop sites with water, such as the Las Vegas Springs in southern Nevada. The Los Angeles *Star* reported on May 31 that 150 Mormon families were at Cajon Pass at the end of the high desert. The San Bernardino Valley immediately below the pass, and some thirty miles from San Gorgonio Pass to the lower deserts to the east, met the Mormons' logistic requirements for the major staging area. Also, the site would be insulated by many miles of semi-arid country from the gentiles in Los Angeles.

The location selected for the Mormon settlement was Rancho San Bernardino, owned by Diego Sepulveda and the Lugo family. The land was well watered and timber was available in the nearby mountains. The Mormons bought 35,000 acres for about $75,000 from the Californios. This rancho, along with Rancho Jurupa to the south, had been the eastern frontier outposts for the South Coast from the days of Spanish rule; and with the breakdown of the Spanish military frontier control, they bore the initial brunt of the Indian raids coming down Cajon and San Gorgonio Passes. Perhaps, at a little over two dollars an acre, the Californios considered it a cheap price to have an aggressive and cohesive group such as the Mormons as a buffer on their eastern borders.

In building the town of San Bernardino, the general pattern of life in Salt Lake City was followed, with the same disciplined energy and ability. Orchards and vineyards were started, and flour and saw mills were built. Neighbors helped each other in the planting and construction. Other than the tithe, each man retained everything he earned, and the community prospered. Routine wagon trains made the long trek to Utah. Butter, eggs, poultry and lumber were sold in Los Angeles—three or more days away by wagon. Eggs cost the Los Angeles merchants fifteen cents a dozen, and chickens were twenty-five cents apiece. In contrast to Utah's relations with gentiles, the San Bernardino Mormons got along well with the Californios and the Americans who had settled in southern California.

By 1858 much of Brigham Young's vision for his powerful

southern California outpost was far on the way to becoming a reality. In retrospect, with the disintegration of the Californio economy and deserted pasture lands a few years later, the highly organized and motivated Mormons could well have moved into the vacuum and taken control of southern California and had another Mormon state. But none of this was to be. Relationships between the Mormons and the gentiles in Utah went from bad to worse. Threats and counterthreats were made, and ugly incidents occurred. President Buchanan ordered Federal troops into Utah. The Mountain Meadow massacre solidified national public opinion against the Mormons. With his church under attack from all sides, Brigham Young ordered home to Utah the entire community of San Bernardino and the Nevada settlements of Carson Valley and Las Vegas. His orders were obeyed immediately. To the amazement of the Californios and the residents of Los Angeles, the long trek from San Bernardino to Salt Lake City was underway in a few days. Property and land were sold at almost any price. Unsold personal property which could not be taken in the wagons was left to those who wanted it. Over 90 per cent of the 3000 Mormons obeyed their leader's orders without question, as those who remained automatically became apostates from the church. The Mormon influence was ended in southern California. But of greater importance, this community was the first to demonstrate that a strong and prosperous agricultural economy could be established on the South Coast in a period of a very few years. The Mormon experience did not go unnoticed.

A group of German immigrants in San Francisco had heard of the success of the Mormon settlement in San Bernardino. Bound together by language and cultural ties, and disliking the carnival atmosphere of San Francisco, they determined in 1857 to establish a group agricultural venture in southern California, modeled in many ways on the Mormon experience. The colony they founded served as a prototype for agricultural production on the South Coast for the next fifty years.

Each of the German immigrant families subscribed $750 to the joint venture. George Hansen (afterwards the colony superintendent) headed a committee to investigate the availability of good land. The committee bought about 1200 acres of land from Don Pacifico Onteveras at the crossroads of the freight trails from San Pedro to Salt Lake City, and from Los Angeles to San Diego. The acreage formed a block about one and one-quarter miles square, some three miles from the Santa Ana River and five miles from the hacienda of Don Bernardo Yorba, whose daughter had married a German immigrant. Don Bernardo was helpful in the early days of the colony. Among other things, his vaqueros kept the wandering stock off the newly fenced and planted lands of the settlers.

George Hansen laid out a townsite and fifty lots, each of twenty acres. Fencing was started immediately with 40,000 to 50,000 willow cuttings set two feet deep in the ground on the perimeter and other boundaries. The cuttings were strengthened by three horizontal poles, tied to the cuttings with rawhide. There were five and one-half miles of perimeter and thirty-five miles of inside fencing, with four gates into the area which could be locked at night. This was the first large-scale fencing project in southern California, an important investment for settlers in cattle country. In later years a standard statement of the land boomer or real estate salesman was that anything grew on the South Coast. It was certainly true of the colony's planting of willow cuttings. Eventually, the willow trees had to be uprooted because they were using too much irrigation water.

In addition to a cattle fence, a systematic water supply was of paramount importance to the German colony. A main canal, over six miles long, was dug from the Santa Ana River, and 350 miles of ditches distributed the irrigation water through the twenty-acre parcels. In spite of the gophers, the plague of all earthen canals in southern California, the canal successfully delivered the water to the feeder ditches. This was the first major project for agricultural irrigation since the time of the missions. Tens of thousands of grapevines were set out, and the colony called itself the Los Angeles Vineyard Company.

In 1860, three years after the initiation of the venture, the major move of the group from San Francisco took place. The settlers called their new home Anaheim, a combination of the Spanish word *Ana* and the German word *heim*, for home. During the three-year waiting period each family was assessed an additional $750. A committee then arrived at a valuation of each twenty-acre plot as to location and soil and assigned a value of $600 to $1400 to each parcel of land. A parcel number was drawn by lot by each family. If the parcel number showed property valued at $1400, the family paid the company $200. If it was a $600 parcel, the family was returned $600 in cash.

The devotion and energy of the Mormons in founding San Bernardino was certainly equaled by the Anaheim settlers. The building of the wooden houses was a community project. Building materials were bought in quantity from San Francisco and eastern sources. Phineas Banning was pained to discover he was not quite the transportation czar of the South Coast that he had envisaged himself. The Anaheim settlers decided they would have their own Anaheim Landing with a warehouse a few miles south of Wilmington, their own lighters to ships in the roadstead, and their own freight wagons on a well-drained dirt road from the landing to Anaheim. It would not be an overstatement to say Anaheim and San Bernardino were the antithesis of Los Angeles during the 1850s, including the food. A menu of Anaheim's Planters' Hotel, hopefully changed every sixty days, was:

BREAKFAST	Steak Mutton Chop Pork Chop
DINNER	Mutton Chop Steak Pork Chop
SUPPER	Pork Chop Steak Mutton Chop
VEGETABLES EACH MEAL	Potatoes with hides on Carrots, Boiled Onions Garlic Hash

The ingredients of the garlic hash were not identified in this 1865 hotel menu. Under any circumstances, South Coast guests must have wished it was Californio cooking instead.

Well before the actual shooting started in the Civil War, California and western Nevada with its gold and silver had been recognized as a rich prize by both sides. The bulk of public opinion in California was for the Union, particularly in the populous areas around San Francisco and Sacramento. The situation was the reverse in the distant and thinly populated cow counties of southern California, which in the main supported the Confederacy throughout the war. Many of the Americans on the South Coast had emigrated from the seceding states; the El Monte settlers were typical. Further, among the Californios, there was the strong belief that southern California would have become a separate territory after approval by the state legislature and the people in 1859 if the bill had not been opposed in the Congress by the antislavery states.

The news of the attack on Fort Sumter in 1861 took twelve days by pony express to reach San Francisco. The transcontinental telegraph was still six months from completion. However, the new telegraph line was working from San Francisco to Los Angeles, where the news was received with much enthusiasm for what was generally believed to be the start of a short ninety-day war and victory for the Confederacy. General Albert Sidney Johnston, who had married a sister of Dr. John S. Griffin and who maintained a home in Los Angeles, was not so sanguine. Johnston, a Southerner, was in charge of the Army's Department of the Pacific with headquarters in San Francisco. He resigned his commission and rode to Los Angeles, where a group of volunteers for the Confederacy had begun to assemble, and a party of about a hundred men started east by the Butterfield stage route. However, Union troops had been alerted at Fort Yuma and a good many of the group were intercepted. Johnston got through. He was killed two years later fighting Grant at the Battle of Shiloh.

Sixteen thousand California men were mustered into the Union Army during the duration of the war, with most of them assigned to duty in the state itself. Because of California's geographical remoteness, the Lincoln administration remained concerned as to a political coup or disorders in the state as well as successful plots to capture or scuttle gold and silver shipments moving by sea and land to the East. Two regiments did see action with the main Union armies, and the California Column fought small engagements in Arizona, New Mexico and western Texas.

Phineas Banning's judgment and sales ability in establishing a port facility at Wilmington were further buttressed with the Army's decision to build a quartermaster depot there shortly before the outbreak of the Civil War. The depot was to supply the interior posts and was called Drum Barracks after Adjutant General Richard Drum. More than a million dollars was spent over the war years for facility construction, with lumber being brought around the Horn. Munitions and provisions of all kinds were sent from the supply depot to troops in southern California, Utah, Fort Yuma, Tucson and New Mexico.

With the amount of dissidence against the Union and support of the Confederacy, Drum Barracks, along with Fort Latham at Rancho Ballona, developed into a major military establishment, having a total of 3000 troops based on the South Coast in a civilian population of considerably less than 15,000. As a part of the buildup, the troops at Fort Tejon were moved to the Los Angeles area. With rumors that Confederacy sympathizers were using gold and silver prospecting as a front to take over Catalina Island, a company of infantry was sent to the Isthmus in early 1864; barracks were built; and the entire island placed under military control. Actually, southern California limited its support of the Confederate cause to volunteers who went east, strong vocal expressions, and occasional personal brawls at home. That the dearly loved Fourth of July celebrations were not held during the war years showed as much as anything the depth of general feeling for the Confederacy.

The Army detailed Lieutenant E. F. Beale to bring about

thirty-five camels to Fort Tejon from the Rio Grande in 1857. Jefferson Davis, as Secretary of War, felt the camel would be an ideal military vehicle for the deserts of the Southwest. At his direction, a herd of camels was brought to Texas from Egypt and Arabia, along with some camel drivers. Half of the herd was sent to California under Beale's direction, with the remainder allocated to the Territory of New Mexico, which included Arizona. During the Civil War Beale's camels were based at Los Angeles and Wilmington, with camel expresses going to Tucson and Fort Mojave. The Army sold the camels after the war, and twenty-five of them were used on a Nevada ranch for a time to transport salt to grinding mills. Fifty years later, and long after the Civil War camel episode had been forgotten, there would be people who would heatedly testify they saw a wild camel silhouetted against the skyline of a desert mountain. Perhaps they did.

Wilmington prospered during the Civil War, growing to 6000 people, including the troops stationed there. For a while it seemed reasonable that this should be the chief center of the South Coast, and Phineas Banning, the town's founder, did not discourage this idea. Los Angeles also benefited from the commercial activity and the military purchase of supplies, to say nothing of payroll moneys spent by soldiers in Calle de Los Negros.

The news in 1865 that the Civil War had ended was received with limited real jubilation in southern California. The report which followed of Abraham Lincoln's assassination even met with enthusiasm in some quarters. Dr. John S. Griffin, a strong Southern supporter, was dining at Harris Newmark's home, when a man came running down the street shouting the news of the assassination, which had just come over the telegraph wire from San Francisco. Griffin "was on his feet instantly, cheering for Jeff Davis . . . and hurrahing for the Confederacy"[1] and headed for the door to the street. Newmark held him back by main force, "convincing him at last of his folly."[2]

There were a number of reasons why the end of the war was not a cause of celebration for the South Coast: the area had suffered few casualties on either side of the bloody war other than in the ranks of volunteers who had gone east; the Confederacy had strong support among groups of former Southerners; and a major military base would shortly be closed, ending its large monetary contributions to the South Coast. The basic cattle economy of the region had been reeling under a series of blows for a number of years and was now nearly moribund. Returning unsupported to this pastoral life was a bleak prospect.

CHAPTER 9

"Thousands of carcasses
strew the plains"

"The flush times are passed—the days of the large prices and full pockets are gone."[1] The *Star's* editorial comment in 1856 was more or less accurate. The cattle herds of the Texas and Missouri frontiers were moving into the San Francisco and Sacramento markets, and local herds in the bay areas were being built up. The selling price for a head of cattle on the South Coast was less than half of what it had been several years before. On the other hand, it was still three times what it had been before the Gold Rush.

Herds were still driven north from the South Coast, but again the Californios began to make carne seca, or dried beef, for export at an operating profit. Carne seca was long a Californio food staple, and before the Gold Rush, it had been exported, along with hides and tallow. Robert G. Cleland described the process for making the dried beef:

> When a steer was killed, the hide was spread out, hair-side down, and used as a receptacle for the meat. The latter, cut into strips about an inch thick, and from one to three feet long, was dipped in brine, hung on a rawhide rope, in the hot sun, and turned every twenty-four hours. In four or five days the meat was hard, black and dry. It was then made into fifty- or sixty-pound bales and bound together with pieces of rawhide. . . . "The mode of cooking dried beef," wrote [Abel] Stearns, "is to pound it up fine and then put it into a pan with a little hot lard, stir and moisten with a little water. A little boiled potato, & onion cut fine, with a little red chile & tomato mixed with it makes a very fine dish. . . ."[2]

The export of carne seca, tallow and hides appeared to be a sound business at the prices prevailing after the cattle boom.

The indefatigable Phineas Banning formed a partnership with A. F. Hinchman to process the ranchos' cattle in quantity—the South Coast's first meat-packing house. There was general agreement at the time on the dollar numbers both for the selling prices of the products of a full-grown steer and for the direct processing costs:

TOTAL SELLING PRICE FOR PRODUCTS OF A FULL-GROWN STEER $12.75

Selling Price by Product

Hide ($2 to $3)	$2	
Tallow (200 lbs @ 4¢ lb.)	8	
Carne Seca (50 lbs @ 5¢-6¢ lb)	2.75	

Processing Costs (including processor's profit) $4.50

Cost Elements
$5 a cord of wood
$5 a day for chief butcher
70¢ a day for each Indian
$2 to Indian supervisor and recruiter

Residual Amount for Rancho Expenses and Profit $ 8.25

Assuming an $8.25 average residual amount for rancho costs and profits from processing a full-grown steer, a rancho as an operating business should have done well. Prior to 1849 the selling price for the steer products seldom exceeded four dollars. Other than the increased standard of living of the Californios themselves, the only major economic factors added after the Gold Rush were increased direct taxes and continuing litigation costs connected with proving land patents.

The Mexican government of Alta California prior to annexation by the United States obtained its limited revenues from custom duties and port charges, which, of course, were reflected in the selling prices of cattle products and manufactured goods. The Americans introduced the general property tax, the prime source of revenue for the local governments as well as the state.

While the Californios in the 1850s felt strongly that the state legislature, dominated by the commercial and mining interests of northern California, would impose confiscatory property tax rates on the large landholdings of the South Coast, the record did not bear out their fears. Rather there were bitter accusations by settlers in the southern cow counties that large quantities of land and thousands of cattle were never entered on the assessment rolls because of the influence of the Californios at the county government level. Undoubtedly there was truth in these charges, particularly so far as cattle were concerned. Certainly, in Arizona and New Mexico of the present-day era, there has been a substantial discrepancy between the total number of cattle carried on the assessment rolls of the counties and the number of cattle for the same areas reported by the U.S. Department of Agriculture in its livestock reports. In 1856, the wealthiest landowner on the South Coast, Don Abel Stearns, paid total state and local property taxes of about $1450 on three of his ranchos (Los Alamitos, Las Bolsas and Los Coyotes, totaling 37,000 acres) and his personal property, principally cattle and livestock. Even with cattle prices half what they were during the boom period, this was scarcely an onerous burden.

Litigation costs for proving patents on rancho land was a factor with which the Californios had to contend, along with property taxes of American rule. Henry W. Halleck, who handled more of the land-patent cases for the Californios than any other lawyer, charged an overall average fee of two and a half cents an acre plus expenses which could easily be several thousand dollars or more. However, the United States Land Commission finished all of its hearings by coincidence shortly after the cattle boom ended, and a good portion of the land litigation expenses should have been paid by the Californios during "the days of the large prices and full pockets."[3] But on a number of occasions Halleck and other responsible lawyers like him had difficulty in collecting their fees even in the good times.

The Californios were improvident when they had the hard cash in their hands for the immediate years after the Gold Rush. The new property taxes and land-patent litigation costs were fixed charges which could have been handled from the operating revenues of the ranchos both during and after the cattle boom.

Instead, the Californios spent their money on a recklessly high standard of living and borrowed money at ridiculous compound-interest rates with little real thought as to how, if ever, the loans and interest would be paid. At a low interest rate for those days of 3 per cent interest a *month,* a debt of $3445.37 could be $58,750 eight years later, as Julio Verdugo found out when he mortgaged his tenant-in-common interest in Rancho San Rafael.

Cattle prices continued to fall but at a slower rate through the end of the 1850s. John G. Downey wrote a special California section for the 1860 Census agricultural report in which he said: " . . . we now have in the state three million horned cattle, a number far beyond the wants of consumption . . . this branch of the industry has become . . . ruinous."[4] The worst was yet to come for the Californios of the South Coast—first a flood and then drought and smallpox.

The arrival of the first substantial rainstorm in the fall of the year was always a major event in the cattle economy of southern California. With little or no rain since the previous spring, the countryside was parched, brown and dusty, with large aimless cracks in the adobe clay ground. In a matter of a few weeks after the first heavy rain in late October or early November the yearly miracle of change took place. The green hills and valleys stretched to the gaunt mountains with their caps of snow. The clay cracks healed, and the stream beds filled with water. With normal rainfall spread over the six-month period of late fall to early spring it was superb cattle country. The herds had the luxuriant grass during the rainy period and adequate pasturage in the bottom lands with burr clover and alfilaria in the uplands during the dry season.

However, the cattle economy of the Californios was always in a precarious climatic balance. The rains came from the major Pacific storms which swept routinely over Washington, Oregon and the extreme northern part of California. Southern California was on the erratic fringe of this winter storm pattern. As a result, on a chance basis there could be scant rainfall over the critical six-month period or much of it could be concentrated in a short period of days or weeks. For well over a two-year period beginning in early 1862, southern California was destined to go through a terrible drought immediately preceded by a major flood.

A great Pacific storm struck the California coast in 1861 shortly before the Las Pastores Christmas celebrations on the South Coast. The storm remained stationary for a time because of a massive atmospheric pressure ridge to the east. The rain poured down, particularly north of the Tehachapi Mountains. Another and another storm system followed, with heavy rain falling almost constantly for nearly a month. With about thirty-five inches of rain during January and February of 1862, flooding in the great interior valleys of northern California was extensive. The lowlands were turned into vast lakes, with dead animals, wreckage and debris drifting in the mindless currents of the flooded areas.

The water poured off the bare-rock mountains of southern California into the valleys and plains below. Hills were cut with new arroyos and gulches, many of them dozens of feet deep. Rivers found new beds, and low-lying lands were flooded to the highest point in memory. Transportation other than horse-back was impossible. Even travel by horse was difficult and dangerous with washed-out trails and rattlesnakes driven down by the floods. As the Los Angeles *Star* reported despondently on January 25, 1862: "Another week has passed without mail, making five consecutive weeks, during which we have had no communication with the outer world, except by steamer express."[5] With a continuing pattern of southeast gales, there was little steamer traffic. Adobe buildings in Los Angeles began to crumble, and merchants watched morosely as the walls softly collapsed on their goods, showcases and shelves. Shopkeepers in the new brick Arcadia Block were the envy of the less fortunate. The water was four feet deep in the streets of the Anaheim settlement.

Finally the torrential rains ended; they were to be the last real rainfall for over two years. Pasturage for herds was excellent, and the cattle were fat for a time. However, the grass browned early in the spring because there was little precipitation after the deluge of late December and January. The rains did not come in the fall and winter of 1862-63. C. R. Johnson wrote Don Abel Stearns in February " . . . there is no grass and the cattle are very poor; your Rancho men report a great many dying. . . . "6 This was only the beginning. The wet season ended in April with about one-quarter of the normal rainfall for the period. With the drought there were the hot dry santana winds blowing persistently off the deserts and carrying hordes of grasshoppers which stripped the scanty forage, crops, vine-yards and orchards.

Along with the blustery santana winds came smallpox. To add to the burdens of the Californios, a virulent epidemic spread throughout the South Coast. It struck with equal severity at the isolated ranchos and at Los Angeles, leaving in its wake despair and horror reminiscent of the plagues of the Middle Ages. Vaqueros were posted day and night at the approaches to the ranchos to warn off strangers, as word spread that in the little town of Los Angeles with a population of less than 5000 as many as fifteen or twenty people were dying a day. Undertakers were refusing to bury the dead, and the Common Council stopped the constant tolling of church bells. Vaccines could be obtained only from San Francisco and received only limited use. There were few doctors and even less understanding of the prevention of the disease by the people. The epidemic finally ran its miserable course, and the Californios waited with quiet desperation for the fall and winter rains of 1863-64.

Again the rains did not come, but the dry santana winds from the deserts did. The weakened stock died by the thousands, piled in heaps by sanded-up waterholes or pulled down by coyotes, bears and mountain lions. The *Los Angeles News* of January 22, 1864, reported: "The cattle of Los Angeles County are dying so fast in many places that the large ranchos keep their men busily employed in obtaining hides. Thousands of carcasses strew the plains in all directions, a short distance from this city, and the sight is harrowing in the extreme. . . . "7 The news article neglected to mention the stench of the decaying carcasses under the brassy skies as well as the pall of smoke and blowing ashes from brush and forest fires in the surrounding parched hills and mountains.

The normal fall and winter rains arrived in the 1864-65 season. It was too late. Over 70 per cent of the cattle herds of the South Coast had been destroyed. Notwithstanding a drastically reduced assessed valuation on range lands and cattle, the Californios had no money to pay their taxes or the mortgage loans, and five-sixths of the property of Los Angeles County was on the delinquent tax rolls. Much of the remaining cattle on the ranges was sold at tax and foreclosure auctions.

Even shrewd and wealthy Abel Stearns found himself in desperate financial trouble. Leverage-wise, he had seriously overextended himself and was caught in a liquidity squeeze. For five years it was a knife-edge balance as to whether he would lose everything. Stearns' travail, described by Robert G. Cleland, was the pattern for the other large landholders:

> As financial and business conditions grew worse throughout southern California, demands poured in on Stearns from every quarter. One of his lawyers, unable "to get a cent from him" on account, threatened to bring suit to collect a bill for $1800; several notes on which both principal and interest had long been in default were presented for payment; and one of his agents plaintively wrote, "There are so many demands for money . . . but I do the best I can." . . . Among the most pressing of his obligations was a note for $35,000 owing to John Parrott of San Francisco. . . . Parrott sued out a writ of attachment against 3000 of Don Abel's horses and 15,000 of his cattle. Though some attempt was made to avoid a forced sale of stock, Parrott soon grew impatient with what he called Stearns' "procastinating system of doing business"; scolded him for refusing to accept advice; and finally instructed the sheriff to enforce the writ. As a result of this action, there was such an "awful sacrifice" of livestock that one of Stearns' representatives doubted if "anything could be saved, either for Don Abel or his creditors." . . . Time after time his ranchos were advertised for sale at public auction, to meet the most inconsequential sums: $91.35

on the eight-square league Rancho La Habra; $91.35 on the eight-square league Rancho Las Bolsas; $12.10 on his interest in the Rancho Cajon de Santa Ana; $81.90 on the Rancho Laguna.[8]

It seemed impossible for Abel Stearns to hold onto any of his property. Rancho Alamitos was taken over by Michael Reese in 1865. The court issued a decree of foreclosure on Arcadia Block in 1867. Stearns' 1868 net annual income was less than $300. With the revival of business conditions and almost literally at the last moment, he was able to get a $43,000 loan in 1868 from the Hibernia Loan and Savings Society in San Francisco in return for a blanket mortgage on all his ranchos. The money saved him from bankruptcy. His longer-term financial salvation depended on the success of the plan of his old friend Alfred Robinson, who proposed to have a national promotion and sale of Stearns' holdings to small settlers.

In contrast to his Californio friends, Abel Stearns had the tremendous advantages of English-language fluency, financial knowledge and widespread contacts in California and the rest of the United States. If Stearns was in desperate financial difficulties during and after the great drought, it is easy to envisage what happened to the rest of the Californios' ranchos during this period. There was one notable exception—Manual Dominguez and Rancho San Pedro.

Don Manuel Dominguez was buried from the St. Vibiana Cathedral in Los Angeles on October 13, 1882. In the old tradition, engraved invitations were sent for his funeral and burial in the new Calvary Cemetery on the east side of the city. He was seventy-nine when he died in his hacienda at Rancho San Pedro, an affluent and powerful Californio still. Medical and burial expenses as shown in probate records of the estate (including $1000 to the Plaza Church for special masses) amounted to $3455, a significant sum for that day.

The old Don had accomplished what no other Californio had been able to do. He had held his ancestral lands of 28,000 acres intact through the misfortunes and vicissitudes of the 1850s and 1860s.

Manuel Dominguez stayed out of debt and managed the rancho affairs himself. He personally supervised the transfer of cattle which had been sold and kept his own tally along with that of the buyer's agent. Any buyer knew that Manuel Dominguez's cattle was purchased with gold. If the price per head was twenty dollars, as each animal was tallied, a twenty-dollar gold piece was expected to be dropped into Dominguez's chamois money pouch. Many an agent found Don Manuel's temper was short-fused. His profanity in both breadth and depth enjoyed a considerable reputation on the South Coast. Initially, it was in Spanish, but as the years passed, the profanity became a peculiarly devastating blend of Spanish and English. A reporter for the San Francisco *Alta California* was impressed in 1869 with the head of the Dominguez family:

> There is one tough old customer left, old Manuel Dominguez, who owns leagues and leagues of land on the sea, extending back nearly to Los Angeles. His possessions extend further than the eye can reach, and he won't sell an acre. There he sits in his lonely grandeur, defying alike taxes, Yankees, and compound interest; nothing can induce him to sell. He has been offered a million, but no, in choicest Spanish he will see them in . . . etc., etc., the gay old duffer.[9]

Don Manuel Dominguez was certainly a man to be reckoned with and decidedly atypical of the Californios on business matters.

From 1859 to 1865 the total assessed property valuation of Los Angeles County *dropped* 65 per cent. With the cattle herds decimated by drought and much of the remainder glutting the markets with tax and foreclosure auctions, the Californios had only their vacant range lands to raise money for their debts. There were few buyers for the lands. Cloudy titles, ill-defined boundaries and tenant-in-common disputes made litigation expensive and inevitable for a prospective buyer. The ranchos disappeared into other hands by foreclosure. "On the assessor's lists their broad leagues of grazing lands dwindled in size to fifty-vara lots, planted to tiny milpas of beans, melons and chili peppers."[10]

The story of deserted cattle ranges and a brave and generous people ending a way of living is not pleasant. But the nature of life means that there always is an end and then a beginning. Events were already under way to give the South Coast a new beginning.

PART TWO

CHAPTER 10

"If we can't pay
a thousand men,
we'll hire only five hundred"

The Civil War set in motion two events which affected the South Coast for a generation. With the dislocations at the end of the war there was a major tide of emigration from the Southern and Border states to the West. A good many settlers came to the South Coast as a result. The other and probably more important action triggered by the Civil War was the signature of Abraham Lincoln on the Pacific Railroad Bill in 1862. Then, with the long-discussed railroad moving from fantasy to fact, four men—Huntington, Stanford, Hopkins and Crocker (the Big Four)—would go a long way toward controlling the destiny of the South Coast and, for that matter, much of California.

Construction began on the Pacific railroad in 1862. The Americans in California had listened seriously to the dreams and plans of such a railroad to the East by enthusiasts like Theodore Judah years before. Their strong feeling of isolation from home and family thousands of miles away was of equal importance to the obvious need for faster and better transportation in the West. Coupled with all of this was the plain fascination of the new mode of transportation. The thought of traveling in an hour the distance which would require a long and exhausting day by prairie schooner was tangible evidence to them of a new era of progress; and the wood-burning locomotive puffing large quantities of smoke and spewing sparks from its high diamond-shaped stack was the fire-breathing symbol of all of this. Each of the little engines had a name. Its hauling power and speed were ordinary subjects of saloon and household discussion. Sheet-music railroad songs were guaranteed to sell. Henry George, a year before the completion of the Pacific railroad, reflected the enthusiasm of the times: " . . . it will be the means of converting a wilderness into a populous empire in less time than many of the cathedrals of Europe were building."[1] In short, California expected the best of all worlds from the new road.

Any self-respecting politician in the West prior to the Civil War always had a few ringing speeches in his election campaign about the absolute need for a Pacific railroad from the Mississippi River. It was campaign talk. There was no money; no feasible route had been surveyed; and men like Daniel Webster had set the national tone in the 1840s:

"What do we want with . . . this region of savages and wild beasts, of deserts of shifting sands and whirlwinds of dust, of cactus and prairie dogs, To what use could we put those endless mountain ranges? What could we do with the Western Coast of three thousand miles, rockbound, cheerless and uninviting?"[2]

Webster's eloquence and feelings hardly reflected a driving expression of manifest destiny or a financial climate for the building of an expensive railroad. Two interlocked factors changed all of this—gold and silver discoveries in the West and then the Civil War.

The Pacific Railroad Convention met in San Francisco in 1859. The purpose of the meeting was to arrive at some position or posture as to what California would do financially for a Pacific railroad and what would be required from the Federal Government. Seven years earlier, as a minor sop to the West, the Congress had authorized the Secretary of War to locate the most economical and practical route for a railroad to the Pacific from the Mississippi River. The result was a series of well-bound bulky reports which dealt in generalities along with expositions of the fauna and flora of the West. The reports were well tuned to the no-action temper of the Congress during that period.

Theodore Judah was a persuasive delegate to the Pacific Railroad Convention in San Francisco, and he had done his homework on feasible routes for the proposed road. In another generation he would have had a scientific Ph.D. with solid engineering knowledge and been known as a great technical salesman. The convention made a wise decision and sent Judah to Washington to lobby for the railroad. When the Congress and Abraham Lincoln needed the gold and silver of the West to fight the Civil War, Judah was there with an engineering and operating plan. The years of lobbying work paid off. Notwithstanding the dislocations of vacant desks and open committee assignment caused by the departure of its Southern members, the Congress moved on the Pacific railroad, and President Lincoln signed the bill on July 1, 1862. Judah sent a telegraph message west to his associates, four of whom would dominate much of California for a generation: "We have drawn the elephant. Now let us see if we can harness him up."[3] Judah and his California associates had drawn a very large and powerful elephant with an irascible and uncertain temperament. One look at the towering and forbidding Sierras to the east of Sacramento would demonstrate that.

The congressional act, as summarized by Oscar Lewis, designated two companies to build and operate a railroad between Sacramento and the Missouri River. In the way of Federal aid it granted a strip of land for right-of-way purposes and made further grants of ten alternate 640-acre sections per mile of public domain (with unimportant exceptions) on both sides of the line over the entire distance. Further, it provided for a government loan to each of the companies, in the form of thirty-year bonds at 6 per cent interest, in an amount ranging from $16,000 to $48,000 per mile, depending on the nature of the territory over which the road would pass.

The company building westward from the Missouri finally got itself organized fourteen months after Lincoln signed the railroad bill. It called itself the Union Pacific, with the key promoters being T. C. Durant and Henry Farnum. Judah and his partners, who would build eastward from Sacramento, were well ahead of their Union Pacific competition. Their proposed railroad, organized as a company just before the bill was signed, was called the Central Pacific. Leland Stanford was president; Collis P. Huntington, vice president; James Bailey, secretary; Mark Hopkins, treasurer; and Theodore Judah, chief engineer. Charles Crocker would shortly be a vice president, and Judah and Bailey would be out. Judah's detailed engineering survey for the first element of the Central Pacific eastward out of Sacramento was completed about three months after the congressional bill was signed into law, and roadbed grading got under way.

Wall Street has long said that it will take a lucky manager over a good manager any day of the week. The Big Four— Huntington, Stanford, Crocker and Hopkins—as a managing group were unusual. They were at the right place at the right time, and, as a managing group, each buttressed the others' weaknesses whether they individually recognized it or not. Huntington, who had an acid tongue, once said that Stanford's share of the building of the railroad consisted in turning the first shovelful of earth and driving the last spike. Huntington was completely convinced that the entire workload of the enterprise was on his shoulders and that naturally the eventual success was due solely to his efforts. Hopkins, a taciturn man, certainly felt his financial controls, sound judgment and peace-making efforts between the other three strong personalities were the key ingredients. There was not any question in Crocker's mind at all—he built the railroad. Stanford's position was equally straightforward. He was the salesman; he kept the political fences mended, and after all, he was president of the company. Obviously, none of the four believed that Theodore Judah could contribute anything, which view, of course, was not shared by Judah. On the other hand, James Bailey speedily recognized there was no place for him. The triggering incident was Judah and Bailey's objection to the construction work of the railroad being handled by a firm owned chiefly by the Big Four. The end result was that the Big Four bought out Judah's and Bailey's interests, with Judah expecting to be asked by the Federal Government to take over operations after the Big Four failed.

The four partners had come their separate ways from the New York State area after the Gold Rush and become successful merchants in booming Sacramento. At the time they organized the Central Pacific, Crocker ran a dry goods store; Stanford was a wholesale grocer and had just been elected governor of California; and Huntington and Hopkins were partners in a hardware business. In contrast to most of the newcomers to California they were not young men. Hopkins was nearly forty-nine; Crocker, forty; Huntington, thirty-nine; and Stanford, the new governor, thirty-eight. In the years they had been in the Sacramento area, they had built their business enterprises on the concept of a quick profit and shrewd calculations as to pricing their merchandise to the maximum that the traffic would bear. In many ways it was the basic business and mining philosophy of the gold-field economy: make your money now, corner the market if possible, and let the devil take the hindermost. The partners would carry this formula over into the operation of the railroad. First, however, they had to build the road over some of the most difficult terrain in the world.

The Big Four began to recognize that they had an almost impossible task—with or without Judah. All that the partners had received from the Federal Government was a hunting license to build a railroad which could be exhibited when they were looking for money. The North was losing battle after battle to the South. Lincoln and his generals were under attack. The confidence level of the people putting up hard cash on the basis of eventual Government payout for the railroad was low. The partners had no track record of performance in an operation of this size, and their railroad experience was zero. There was a widespread belief in San Francisco that the Big Four really intended to build a wagon road across the Sierras to monopolize the Nevada silver traffic.

Desperate necessity brought the divergent skills of the four men into full play, and the nature and size of the obstacles to be overcome welded them into a formidable and balanced team. Huntington went to the East Coast to scrounge material, supplies and equipment in the middle of a major and devastating war. He called on the other three men for unlimited power of attorney and blank notes. In other words, Huntington could commit these middle-aged men for every dollar they and their families had. Stanford meanwhile was frantically working on his political alliances and friendships. Within a year the state and various California counties bought stock in the amount of $1,500,000 and agreed to pay interest up to a like amount of the bonds of the Central Pacific. Even San Francisco, which viewed the efforts of the Sacramento shopkeepers with marked coolness, eventually anted up $400,000 as an outright gift. Construction work got under way. Despite Hopkins' rigid financial controls, Crocker's minimal operating requirements for money seemed insatiable. For a period of several weeks there was no money at all to pay bills. Huntington told his partners: "If we can't pay a thousand men, we'll hire only five hundred—if we can't pay five hundred men, we'll hire ten."[4] All of this was while the railhead crawled toward the foothills of the Sierras, and the huge money expenditures still lay ahead. As the amateur railroaders persisted at their task, the entrenched interests began to take them seriously. Stage and freight lines, the Pacific Mail Steamship Company, the existing telegraph company, the Sacramento Valley Railroad and even a company that brought ice to San Francisco from Alaska formed an organized opposition to discredit the financing efforts of the Central Pacific. In a running series of brawls, the partners fought back, with no holds barred.

It was evident to Huntington that the railroad could not be built over the Sierras without increased Federal Government subsidy. Obviously, the first thing to be done was to obtain the maximum favorable interpretation of the 1862 railroad act as to mileage subsidies. The maximum Federal payment rate was $48,000 a mile for mountain terrain. But what was the definition of a mountain? He finally convinced the Government that a mountain subsidy should start seven miles outside Sacramento despite the fact that the valley stretched flat as a billiard table for miles ahead to the mountains. To say the least, cynical

San Francisco was impressed with the ability of the Big Four to move the Sierra Nevadas to within a few miles of Sacramento. After officially moving the mountains, Huntington started serious lobbying in Washington, along with the Union Pacific promoters, for major financing changes in the railroad act. President Lincoln signed a new railroad bill in 1864 which delighted Huntington, who was a hard man to please. Among other things, it made the Government bonds subordinate to a senior debt issue of the company up to the same amount; time limits to reach the California-Nevada line by the Central Pacific were extended to four years; the amount of land-grants acreage was doubled.

Crocker built the railroad with men, one-horse dump carts, black powder, and picks and shovels. The tools at hand were pitifully inadequate to attack the mountain barrier towering to the east in front of him. The High Sierras are new mountains, a great block of granite tilted sharply upward on its eastern side and rising in a few miles to a maximum height of over 14,000 feet at Mount Whitney. While the slope to the west is on a more gradual basis, there are steep canyons cut by brawling streams through the tough granite. Winter snow levels are enormous, far more than in the Rocky Mountains. The water-laden air from the Pacific Ocean dumps huge quantities of snow during the massive winter storms, through rapid adiabatic cooling as the moist air hits the flanks of the high new mountains. Snowfall rate is difficult to believe. In one of the two great winter storms of 1969, the writer saw snow pile up by the foot over a period of hours at Squaw Valley. A ski-lodge parking lot would be cleared in the morning with heavy Sierra snow equipment, and by early evening there would be another five feet of new snow burying parked automobiles above their roofs. This went on for two days. As much as 73 feet of snow has been recorded during a Sierra winter season—this at 8000 feet. Sixty-five feet of snow has been logged in at Donner Pass, the railroad route, with a yearly average of 31 feet. Added to this is the constant threat of avalanches and high winds in the winter which are funneled up the canyons and through the passes. It was an impossible task to build a railroad across these mountains, but Crocker and his crew refused to recognize it.

While Huntington and Stanford finally had solved the money problem, getting labor for the difficult and dangerous construction work was another matter. Only two out of every five recruits reported to the foremen on the job. Most of those who did worked only long enough to earn the stage fare to the Nevada silver fields. Crocker had an idea. When he discussed it with his construction superintendent, James Strobridge, the immediate reaction was strongly negative. Crocker wanted to try Chinese labor. A few thousands of Cantonese men from south China had come to California starting in the early 1850s to do grubbing gold-field work. As time went by they were scattered about California, living completely as aliens in a foreign land. At Crocker's insistence, pilot gangs of Cantonese were hired. Strobridge and Samuel Montague, who had replaced Theodore Judah as chief engineer, were converted as they watched the hard work and amazing endurance of the Chinese. Within six months 2000 of them had been recruited from all over California at a pay rate of forty dollars a month. Crocker decided to increase this force to a maximum of 15,000 men. Ships jammed to the gunwales with Cantonese began to arrive from Hong Kong. By the late 1860s, the first serious mutterings about the "Yellow Peril" were being heard among the white laborers in the state, irrespective of the fact that most of them refused to work on the railroad. Those who did found themselves promoted to rail layers, stoneworkers, powdermen, teamsters and foremen.

As the railroad snaked up the Sierras, Crocker had the makings of a highly effective team. He needed it. Fifteen tunnels had to be punched through granite so hard that the black powder charges sometimes backfired out of the shot hole without even cracking the rock. In 1866, tunnel headings were put underground by late fall. All through the long winter, tunnel blasting followed by pick and shovel work went on by tallow-candle light. Snow tunnels were dug to keep the headings open, but ventilation and the movement of men and supplies was a serious problem. It was no place for a man with claustrophobia. With all of this, the tunnels still inched ahead.

Crocker and his crew were demonstrating that a railroad could be built across the Sierras. But it was equally clear that the railroad could not operate during the winter months with the amount of snow and number of avalanches. Arthur Brown, the building and bridge superintendent, calmly suggested that the Central Pacific build forty miles of snowsheds of very heavy wood and run the railroad through them. Two years and 65,000,000 board feet of lumber later, the job was done. An all-weather route across the Sierras was an accomplished fact. Train crews, as they coughed from the smoke in the sheds, would grumble that it was the first time they had ever railroaded in a forty-mile barn.

The official date that the Big Four had a completed railroad and were potentially rich men was May 10, 1869. At a temporary village called Promontory in Utah and 690 miles from Sacramento, the Central Pacific joined the Union Pacific. The partners had just finished the best years of their lives. Crocker understood this—the others did not.

The Big Four found to their dismay that Theodore Judah's elephant was far from being harnessed after the Pacific railroad was completed in 1869. Having a new railroad is like buying and keeping a very large yacht. The initial cost is high, the maintenance and operations costs are enormous. The rolling stock, rails and roadbed of the new Central Pacific were typical of the day. But they were not suited for the mountainous terrain and high deserts of its route. The "C. P. Huntington," later to be numbered Locomotive No. 1, was twenty-nine and one-half feet long and weighed 43,000 pounds. It was the 4-2-0 type (a four-wheel leading truck, one pair of drivers and no trailing wheels). With a grade of 26 feet to the mile, it would haul four 22-ton cars at perhaps fifteen miles an hour. This was totally inadequate for the route. By the time the railroad was completed, a wood-burning 4-6-0 type with three pair of drive wheels was being used for freight. This locomotive could haul eighteen small freight cars under favorable conditions, but even this improved type was neither efficient nor economical for the rugged terrain.

The iron rails of the road matched the light equipment—fifty-six pounds to the yard. As the heavier rolling stock was introduced, all of the rails required replacement. Tracks had been hastily laid and in many places were spiked to too widely placed crossties. Bridging and other structures were well built, but only expensive experience would show areas of potential washouts and slides. With wood-burning locomotives, fires in the wooden bridge structures and snowsheds were a constant and dollar-consuming problem. Air brakes for the rolling stock had yet to be invented, and the hand-braking by individual car was time-consuming, cumbersome and dangerous on the downgrades and curves. The roadbed was rough and unballasted, and drainage problems caused recurring delays. The only saving grace was that train speeds seldom exceeded twenty miles an hour. Otherwise the casualties among passengers and crew, let alone the loss of scarce and expensive rolling stock and payment of freight claims, would have closed down the railroad.

Other than nearly freezing to death during the winter (there were no steam pipes for heating and no vestibules in the coaches), the passengers found the trip "over the hill," as the railroad people called the Sierras, a memorable experience. So memorable in fact that many of them said vehemently they would never do it again. A cartoon of the period shows a nervous Englishman tapping the shoulder of a very fat miner in the seat ahead and worriedly suggesting: "I say, my man, would you mind leaning toward the *center* on the curves?" The remark seemed particularly apropos at the Cape Horn curve, where the railroad bed was carved and built out of a cliff with a sheer drop of a thousand feet from the tracks to the American River. Once over the 7000-foot Donner Pass and if the train was late for Sacramento, which it usually was, " . . . at what must have seemed a reckless speed, they coasted toward the lowlands, the light coaches swaying around the curves while wheel flanges screamed against the rails, and the friction of the brakes heated the metal shoes until after dark they glowed red-hot, and passengers sniffed nervously at the smell of charring wood beneath their coaches."[5]

The Central Pacific needed very large quantities of money for operation and maintenance. Unfortunately, the West did not have the economic base to provide the money. The Big Four had a national and world curiosity in their railroad with its engineering and construction achievements, so the trains were full of passengers for a while. However, tourist passenger traffic dropped off, and with the opening of the Suez Canal, the expected boom in trade from Europe to the Orient via the Pacific railroad did not materialize. The partners had three choices: sell out; hang on and hope that reasonable freight rates would develop an economic base in the West; or establish a transportation monopoly and charge the maximum the traffic would bear. They made some effort to sell the Central Pacific, but the business panic of 1873 ended that. Meanwhile they chose the monopoly route—a decision which would affect much of California for more than a generation. In retrospect, the Big Four's immediate choice was inevitable. Their background and environment of infighting with any tool at hand and seeking the quick profit by charging the maximum the traffic would bear made such an economic route entirely logical to the Big Four. Combined with their natural drives was a desperate need for money to operate and maintain the raw new railroad. If the partners could make a transportation monopoly work, the money would be forthcoming.

The Big Four moved on three fronts to put a hammerlock on the economy of California. The first priority was to control the railroad and ship transportation of the state. In quick succession Collis P. Huntington made a series of acquisition moves, including a railroad promotion called the Southern Pacific. All things being equal, Huntington preferred the bludgeon approach in buying out his transportation competitors. The purchased companies were folded into a corporation called the Southern Pacific Railroad of California, and transportation rates were raised to the maximum. Concurrent with the acquisition campaign, a pattern of systematic political manipulation and bribery was begun both with the state and local governments and courts. Within a short period of years the Big Four was the government and judicial system of the state on transportation matters. In the process they accumulated a paid-for claque of newspapers scattered throughout California. Some newspapers fought back, including a young editor by the name of Hearst whose family had made a fortune in Comstock silver.

To achieve the maximum return on their monopoly and governmental control, the partners needed settlers near their railroads, which now were all called the Southern Pacific. As the railroads owned alternate 640-acre sections of land along the right-of-way as grants from the Federal Government, sales of this land could be an important source of revenue. A major promotional campaign was launched throughout the United States and in Western Europe as the Southern Pacific moved slowly down the San Joaquin Valley. The campaign in its depth, intensity and planning would have done credit to a major huckstering and tub-thumping campaign of later periods. Advertisements were bought in newspapers, and favorable news articles were planted. A well-organized and well-financed lecture circuit was established throughout the Middle West and the East. The central promotional theme repeated over and over again was the superb climate, wonderful soil and cheap lands of California.

Four and a half years after completion of the Central Pacific, the Big Four's plan for controlling California and filling vacant railroad lands with settlers was beginning to work very well. Mark Hopkins was able to tell his partners that on sales of nearly $14,000,000 in 1873 (a panic year), the company had an operating profit of $8,000,000, a net profit after bond-interest expense of about $5,000,000. With a favorable financial report like this and a future financial picture looking even better, Huntington was ready to make his move.

He had been keeping a cold eye on a southern transcontinental route crossing the Colorado River at Fort Yuma in Arizona Territory or Needles, California, 150 miles north of the fort. While railroad construction had started into and down the San Joaquin Valley by the end of 1869, the Southern Pacific was moving at a leisurely pace to conserve money. Townsites were laid out by the railroad at places like Modesto, Merced, Fresno and Tulare. The rails did not reach Fresno until 1872, and two years later they were at Sumner (now East Bakersfield). By this time the Southern Pacific's financial house was in order even by Huntington's standards.

William Hood, assistant chief engineer, was taken off the leash by Huntington. He was given the go-ahead and the large amount of money required to build the railroad over and through the Tehachapi Mountains, which rose precipitously forty miles south of Bakersfield. This mountain barrier to southern California and the Colorado River was equal in construction problems to the High Sierras, with one major exception—snow was at a minimum. Staring at Hood was the blank face of a mountain at the 1300-foot elevation near a tiny settlement called Caliente. Six miles of railroad and four tunnels later, Hood had progressed south one straight line mile from Caliente. The fifth and largest tunnel was begun and as Neill C. Wilson and Frank J. Taylor describe it:

> Above this No. 5 tunnel, Hood began the first of two giant circles. Into the side of a ridge he burrowed, swung upward, and crossed directly over the point where tunnel No. 9 was just bored. That maneuver gained 77 feet. When the little trains of Hood's day went chugging into the hole and, after a while, crossed directly above their recent point of disappearance, it was spectacular enough, but today's trains add still another quirk. It is not uncommon for the double-header locomotives of a modern freight to be passing over the tunnel just as the caboose of their train flits inside.[6]

While William Hood was building eighteen tunnels in the Tehachapis for the Southern Pacific, Collis P. Huntington was becoming more than annoyed with an upstart South Coast. Conditions had changed there since the terrible days of a decade earlier.

CHAPTER 11

"A tremendously
high figure for dirty,
burry California wool"

The cattle herds of the South Coast were largely destroyed
by the great drought of 1862-64, and most of the Californios
were bankrupt. Because of litigation in the Federal courts, patents or titles to rancho lands were issued ten to twenty years
after the United States Land Commission finished its hearings
in 1856. It was a lawyer's holiday and a landowner's nightmare,
particularly as the squatters moved in. Nobody wanted "to buy a
lawsuit" along with the purchase of vacant range land. The
boundaries of the ranchos were too ill-defined; the titles of the
grants were open to too many questions; and the tenants-in-
common were too many.

Shadows on the titles of ranchos on the South Coast were the
genesis of the present title-insurance industry and with good
reason. As late as the 1920s there was systematic effort to over-
turn the land patents which were finally issued years after the
hearings of the Land Commission were completed. The United
States Senate's Committee on Public Lands and Survey during
Calvin Coolidge's Administration commented in 1927:

> Charges have been made and repeated with frequency that
> vast areas of land in southern California were held under
> fraudulent titles arising from the fact in some instances no
> grant was ever made by the Government of Spain or that of
> Mexico; in some instances forged or fabricated grants have been
> obtained; in some cases grants, although issued subsequent to
> the Treaty of Guadalupe Hidalgo, had been antedated to precede
> American sovereignty, and in other instances a grant was made
> of a fixed quantity of land, but that in surveying and fixing the

boundaries of such a grant, a vast quantity in excess of the
original grant was included in the field notes and the patent
subsequently issued, thus passing into private possession such
excess land which, in fact, is the property of the United States
and constitutes part of the public domain, and, accordingly is
properly subject to homestead entry.[1]

This marvelously complex sentence summarized fairly the
confusion and litigation which existed for many years even after
rancho land patents were issued. The 1927 Senate Committee
and the Coolidge Administration finally took the position that
the successors in interest under the original grants had unques-
tioned legal title. There have been no further title challenges
since the 1920s, but it would not be surprising if there were.

But to a South Coast economy of the 1860s sinking in a
morass of land problems, all of this was no assistance. Nobody
had the courage and money to buy the vacant range land until
men like the Flints, Bixbys and Irvines appeared on the scene.

Flint, Bixby & Co. was organized at the Prairie House in
Terre Haute, Indiana, in 1853, undoubtedly over a meal of
"fried eggs swimming in lard, the almost universal food in this
part of the world."[2] The partnership consisted of three young
Maine men in their late twenties who were driving sheep to
California. Years later they and their large number of relatives
would for a while fill the ranges of the South Coast ranchos
with sheep.

By the middle of the nineteenth century Somerset County,
Maine, was loaded with Bixbys, Westons and a good many
Flints and Hathaways. When Rufus Bixby entertained at Thanks-
giving on one occasion, he had 156 relatives around the table.
The Bixby of Flint, Bixby & Co. was one of an even hundred
of his grandchildren. Many of the Bixbys, Flints, Westons and
some of the Hathaways of that part of Maine arrived in California
over a twenty-five-year period around the time of the Civil War.
With the number of intermarriages between the families, such
as Llewellyn and Jotham Bixby marrying Hathaway sisters, it

required a devoted family historian to sort out the relationships. An outsider who tried to comprehend the interlocking family directorates in their numerous business enterprises could understandably be baffled.

Two brothers, Benjamin and Thomas Flint, and their cousin, Llewellyn Bixby, made some money in California immediately after the Gold Rush, and returned together by sea to the East Coast. There they "united their fortunes for the undertaking of bringing to California sheep and cattle, more for the trip than the profit."[3] Quincy, Illinois, was the jumping-off point in 1853 for their return trip to California with 1800 sheep, eleven yoke of oxen, two cows, four horses, two wagons and four hired hands. At Salt Lake City, they built the flocks up to 2400 head of sheep. The partnership of Flint, Bixby & Co. was no different than a thousand other parties making the long trek across the plains, mountains, and deserts other than the unusual idea of herding a large number of sheep. The partners' destination was central California, but with the inevitable delays and lateness of the season, they decided to go from Salt Lake City to Los Angeles and then up the coast. They had been warned of the difficulties and dangers which a small train moving at a snail's pace would encounter from Salt Lake to San Bernardino on the Mormon Trail. When Colonel John H. Hollister suggested the partners join his party to San Bernardino, they accepted with alacrity, and it was the beginning of a long friendship with the Hollisters. The most difficult portion of the trek on the Mormon Trail, according to Sarah Bixby-Smith writing from Thomas Flint's diary, was a stretch in the Mojave Desert of

> . . . about one hundred miles without water, except for the meager Bitter Water Springs. Most of the wagons and cattle went on ahead, and after three days reached the springs, where they waited for the other men with the sheep. On the fourth day the first of the Hollister sheep came in; on the fifth, in the morning came Ben and father, and in the afternoon Hub Hollister. Dr. Flint mentions the oxen as being "famished for want of food and particularly for water, a sad sight of brute suffering." With the arrival of the sheep the cattle went on to the Mojave River. The sheep did not arrive until the fourteenth, after eleven days

spent in crossing the desert. . . Dr. Flint says: "I packed my horse with provisions and started back to meet Ben and Llewell with the sheep. Met them six miles out. They had used up all their water and food; hence it was a relief to them when I hove in sight. Some of the men had such a dread of the desert that they were beside themselves, imagining they would perish from thirst before getting over the forty miles." . . . After reaching Mojave River they all rested for several days "the men loafing about the camp or pitching horseshoes." . . . They all had a "big fire of cottonwood, which gave a cosy look to the camp." They had a stew of wild ducks and "got a mess of quail for Christmas dinner on the morrow."[4]

On December 30, 1853, the Flint-Bixby party entered Cajon Pass and wound down into San Bernardino, as did so many wagon trains before and after them. To each train it was a fresh miracle to see the flanks of the mountains become wooded and the land turn green. The following spring the partners drove their flocks through San Buenaventura and Paso Robles to San Jose, where they rented pasturage. The next year Flint, Bixby & Co., along with the Hollisters, bought the 54,000-acre Rancho San Justo in Monterey County and aggressively began to expand their flocks of sheep. San Justo would be the partners' headquarters for the next forty years. For fifteen of those years the two Flints and Bixby with their families lived together in one large house, with each of the three wives taking monthly turns in running the huge communal household. Eventually, the Benjamin Flints moved to Oakland and the Bixbys to Los Angeles.

There had been large flocks of sheep during the height of the mission period on the South Coast, although the wool was coarse and mutton was less than a popular meat with the Californios. After the mission breakup in the early 1830s, the number of sheep had dwindled, and most of the remaining flocks had been sold to the mining camps as mutton during the early days of the Gold Rush. Men such as the Flints, Bixbys and Hollisters saw a new business opportunity. From the Middle West they brought in a better grade of sheep which had survived the long overland trek, and pastured the flocks in California under favorable climatic conditions. They expanded their flocks to meet a growing national market for wool caused in part by the heavy northern European immigration to the United States after 1848. With the outbreak of the Civil War and the North's blockade of the Confederacy's cotton, there was a huge demand for wool in the North.

In 1854, the year that Flint, Bixby and Co. sold their first wool, the total wool clip for California was less than 200,000 pounds. A decade later the annual clip was thirty times this amount. The partners could not have chosen a better time to bring their flocks of sheep to California, not only for the trip, as they said in their original partnership agreement, but for most handsome profits. They, along with the Hollisters, were at the epicenter of the wool boom and were eyeing the southern California ranchos for expansion of their flocks.

W. W. Hollister made the first move just after the start of the Civil War when he approached both Pio Pico and Abel Stearns with proposals for leasing or buying some of their acreage on excellent terms. Hollister got nowhere with either of them. Californios as cattlemen did not like sheep on their ranges. This attitude changed abruptly with the drought years of the early 1860s.

John Temple sold his rancho to the newly rich sheepmen in 1866 as his cattle ranges were lying fallow, and he was tired and ill. When Flint, Bixby & Co. offered him $20,000 in gold for the 26,000-acre Rancho Los Cerritos, he accepted. The offer in gold was a major trading point, as greenback currency was still depreciating even though the Civil War was over. This kind of money in gold would buy any land from the hard-pressed Californios. Flint, Bixby & Co. could well afford the Rancho Los Cerritos purchase because California sheep owners during the ten-year boom period for wool were making large profits as their flocks increased.

The partners designated Jotham Bixby, Llewellyn's younger brother who had come around the Horn in 1852, as manager of Los Cerritos, with the option of buying into the ranch at any time. Jotham acquired a half interest in 1869, and the ranch was operated as J. Bixby & Co.

The flocks of sheep were rapidly built up at Los Cerritos to a maximum of 30,000 head, with 200,000 pounds of wool being sent annually to San Francisco. Initially, the wool was shipped from a landing in Newport Bay, but after a few years Wilmington was used as the port. The flocks on the Cerritos range were in clusters of about 2000 head handled by a sheepherder and several dogs. Weekly, the main ranch house sent out food, supplies and mail to the sheep camps. Flour, bacon, beans, potatoes, coffee and brown sugar—the staple camp foods of the American West—went out on the wagons. In the spring and fall the flocks were brought in to the main ranch area to be sheared, dipped and counted. Jotham Bixby supervised the shearing himself and kept his working tallies with knife marks on willow sticks. The vaqueros of the great cattle days were in their last flower during the semi-annual roundups. As shearing began on Monday mornings, the vaqueros arrived on Sunday riding their horses, which had, according to Sarah Bixby-Smith:

> . . . silver-trimmed bridles made of rawhide or braided horsehair, and saddles with high horns, sweeping stirrups, and wide expanse of beautiful tooled leather. The men themselves were dressed in black broadcloth, ruffled white shirts, high-heeled boots, and high-crowned, wide sombreros which were trimmed with silver-braided bands, and held securely in place by a cord under the nose. They would come in, fifty or sixty strong, stake out their caballada, put away their finery, and appear in brown overalls, red bandanas on their heads, and live and work at the ranch for more than a month, so many were the sheep to be sheared. They brought their own blankets and camped out. Their meals were prepared in the cook wagon.[5]

The vaqueros were paid on a piecework basis with copper checks worth five cents redeemed for cash each Saturday. As would be expected, these checks changed hands rapidly during the vaqueros' evening card games.

The main Cerritos ranch house had been built by John Temple in 1844. The adobe structure had a brick foundation and verandahs, with the bricks having been brought around the Horn. The central portion of the house was two-story and a hundred feet long with two long single-story wings connected by a high adobe wall with one gate. The flat roof was typical Californio—redwood planks covered with sand and gravel and overlaid with tar. The lower windows of the structure were iron-barred and loopholes were let into the adobe walls at strategic points for rifle fire. One of the first changes Jotham Bixby made was the installation of a wooden roof of American style on the central portion of the house. He had soon discovered that the Californio roofs leaked in very heavy rains after the tar cracked during the hot dry summers. Another immediate change was the installation of American stoves and cooking. Sarah Bixby-Smith lists a typical day's menu prepared by the Chinese cooks for as many as thirty people:

> At breakfast there was always eggs, or meat,—steaks, chops, sausage—potatoes, hot bread, stewed fruit, doughnuts and cheese and coffee. . . . Dinner came at noon and frequently began with soup, followed by a roast, potatoes, two other fresh vegetables, with pickles, olives and preserves. Salads were unknown, but we sometimes had lettuce leaves, dressed with vinegar and sugar. For dessert there were puddings or pies or cake and home-canned fruit, and cheese. . . . Mush was a supper dish. Sometimes the main article (for supper) was creamed toast, and there might be hot biscuits with jelly, honey or jam, and perhaps cold meat, and always again doughnuts and the constant cheese.[6]

Three times a day the two Chinese cooks put on these kinds of meals for the family and the regular ranch hands, as well as noon lunches for those working away from the main ranch house. It was a good and prosperous American ranch life at Los Cerritos, with the old ways of the Californios rapidly being forgotten.

As time went by, Flint, Bixby & Co., their relatives and friends continued to buy large amounts of southern California land. The partnership and James Irvine of San Francisco had first bought Rancho San Joaquin less than two years before the Los Cerritos purchase. Irvine, a Belfast Irishman, was twenty-two when he joined the Gold Rush to California in 1849, coming up from Panama on the same ship with Benjamin Flint and, incidentally, Collis P. Huntington. During the interminable 101-day passage the two young men started a friendship which lasted over the years. Irvine became a successful commodity merchant in San Francisco and invested his profits in the booming real estate developments of the city. When Flint, Bixby & Co. decided to expand their operations to the empty cattle lands of the South Coast, James Irvine was invited by Benjamin Flint to take a half interest in some of its prospective land investments. The first joint venture was the purchase of the 50,000-acre Rancho San Joaquin from Jose Andres Sepulveda in December of 1864.

The Lugos, the Picos and the Sepulvedas had represented the Californios at their best and worst. Whether it was in courtesy, hospitality, courage, betting or ruinous extravagance during the gold-slug days of the 1850s, these families were in the forefront. It was inevitable that Jose Andres Sepulveda, a second cousin of Jose Loreto Sepulveda of Rancho Los Palos Verdes, would be in financial difficulties as cattle prices dropped sharply in the late fifties, followed by the drought of the early sixties. He had borrowed money from William Wolfskill and others at the prevailing interest rates of 2 to 3½ per cent a month and managed to pay them back. Finally, in October of 1860, he gave a six-month first mortgage on Rancho San Joaquin to Baruch Marks of Los Angeles for $6000 at an interest rate of 2 per cent a month. Shortly thereafter he gave Wolf Kalisher a six-month second mortgage on the property for $5,000. Cattle prices continued to deteriorate, and then the drought and smallpox arrived. Sepulveda managed to continue paying interest for a time on the mortgages, but payment of the principal was out of the question, and then he stopped interest payments also. In 1864 Marks and Kalisher initiated foreclosure proceedings, with a resulting judgment rendered against Sepulveda in the amount of $19,000. Flint, Bixby & Co. and James Irvine bought the Rancho San Joaquin from Sepulveda for $18,000 and "other valuable considerations" in December of 1864 after Sepulveda had found the money to satisfy the judgment. It is reasonable to presume that this money had been advanced by the joint sheep partnership.

The joint venture acquired Rancho Lomas de Santiago from

William Wolfskill the same year Flint, Bixby & Co. bought Los
Cerritos. Wolfskill, along with John Temple and Abel Stearns,
was one of the number of naturalized Mexicans of American
descent in Alta California before the province was ceded to the
United States. He had pioneered the Santa Fe-Los Angeles trade
and married Magdalena Lugo, daughter of Jose Ygnacio Lugo,
in 1841. Wolfskill, in addition to his rancho interests, had been
an early planter of vineyards and citrus on the South Coast. In
1860 he bought the 47,000-acre Rancho Lomas de Santiago from
Teodocio Yorba for $7000. Six years later and just before his
death he sold it to Flint, Bixby & Co. and James Irvine for the
same amount. During that year, the joint partnership also acquired a 3800-acre strip of Rancho Santiago de Santa Ana from
Wolfskill.

With the San Joaquin, Lomas de Santiago and Santiago de
Santa Ana ranches, plus some contiguous purchases, Flint, Bixby
& Co. with James Irvine owned nearly 110,000 acres by the end
of 1866 in what was later Orange Country. Many years after-
wards these holdings would be known throughout California
and the West as the famous Irvine Ranch.

In addition to their ventures with James Irvine on the South
Coast, Flint, Bixby & Co. and their relatives continued to acquire
land. J. Bixby & Co. eventually bought a total of 17,000 acres
(along with the endless litigation) of Rancho Los Palos Verdes.
Jotham Bixby, representing the parent partnership and himself,
began buying these Palos Verdes lands on a piecemeal basis in
the early 1870s from the disintegrating holdings of the Sepulveda
family.

Rancho Alamitos of 26,000 acres was purchased in 1883 by
John W. Bixby, J. Bixby & Co. and Isaias W. Hellman. Abel
Stearns bought Alamitos in 1841 and lost the rancho in 1866 to
Michael Reese when he was in deep financial trouble along with
the rest of the Californios. John Bixby, a cousin of Llewellyn and
Jotham, who had been leasing a thousand or so acres of Alamitos
for five years, wanted the ranch when it came on the market
from Reese's estate. Susan Hathaway Bixby, John's wife, felt he
should do as Jotham Bixby with his J. Bixby & Co. had done

earlier—become a manager of a large ranch and have an interest in it. At her urging: "First he was to see the big Los Angeles banker, I. W. Hellman. He (Hellman) said he would go into the purchase if Jotham Bixby would; the latter said he would if Flint, Bixby & Co. would. They all would and so it came about the Alamitos was secured, Mr. Hellman owning one-third, J. Bixby & Co. another third and young John Bixby in as manager with his third."[7] One would suspect young John had excellent family credentials to present to Hellman, the banker.

Within twenty years after the two Flints and Llewellyn Bixby were throwing horseshoes alongside the Mojave River after crossing the desert with their flocks of starving sheep, they controlled a good portion of the South Coast. The decision of the partnership and James Irvine to acquire huge acreages of South Coast land, cloudy titles or not, encouraged a number of others to buy Californio ranchos to raise sheep and gamble in wool.

Even Harris Newmark, a shrewd commodity merchant and an old-timer, was caught up in the wool boom and speculation. He paid Louis Wolfskill the very large sum of $85,000 for the 6000-acre Rancho Santa Anita in March of 1872. Commenting wryly years later on this ranch acquisition, Newmark said: "In the light of the aftermath, the statement that our expectation of prospective wool profits inspired this purchase seems ludicrous, but it was far from laughable at the time."[8] Newmark goes on to tell of the wild speculation in wool during the period and his own involvement:

> We commenced purchasing on the sheep's back in November, and continued buying everything that was offered until April, 1872, when we made the first shipment, the product being sold at forty-five cents a pound. As far as I am aware the price of wool had never reached fifty cents anywhere in the world, it being ordinarily worth ten to twelve cents. . . . Forty-five cents was a tremendously high figure for dirty, burry, California wool in the grease. . . . I became wool-crazy, the more so since I knew that the particular shipment referred to was of very poor quality.

Colonel R. S. Baker, who was living on his ranch in Kern County, came to Los Angeles about that time, and we offered him fifty cents a pound for Beale & Baker's clip. . . . Beale proved as wool-crazy as I and would not sell.

The brothers Philip, Eugene and Camille Garnier of the Encino Ranch had a clip of wool somewhat exceeding one hundred and fifty thousand pounds. . . . On the same day I made Colonel Baker the offer of fifty cents, I told Eugene I would allow him forty-eight and a half cents for the Garnier product. This offer he disdainfully refused. . . . I do not believe that in my entire commercial experience I ever witnessed anything demonstrating so thoroughly, as did these wool transactions, the monstrous greed of man. . . . My offer to the Garnier Brothers was made on Friday. During that day and the next, we received several telegrams indicating that the crest of the craze had been reached, and that buyers refused to take hold. On the Monday following the first visit of Eugene Garnier, he again came to town and wanted me to buy their wool at the price I had quoted him on Friday; but by that time we had withdrawn from the market. . . . The Garnier Brothers shipped their product East and, after holding it practically a full year, finally sold it for sixteen and a half cents a pound in currency, which was then worth eighty-five cents on the dollar. The year 1872 is on record as the most disastrous wool season in our history, when millions were lost; and H. Newmark & Company suffered their share in the disaster.[9]

After the drop of wool prices that Newmark described, Flint, Bixby & Co. took a hard look at their extensive landholdings on the South Coast as well as in Central California. James Irvine, their partner in the San Joaquin, Lomas de Santiago and Santiago de Santa Ana complex, had become an enthusiast on the future business opportunities on the South Coast, and he had the cash to support his views. On the other hand, the partnership decided it was land-poor. Irvine and Flint, Bixby & Co. made a deal in 1876: Irvine would buy out the partners' half interest in the ranch complex of San Joaquin, Santiago and Santa Ana for $150,000.

From a near-term viewpoint, the partnership's decision to sell the holdings to James Irvine was beautifully timed. A year after the sale the thriving sheep industry in southern California came to an abrupt end. Its demise was almost identical to the end of the cattle period some years earlier. California wool prices continued to be depressed after 1872. The rains did not come in the winter season of 1876-77, but smallpox did. The sheep died by the thousands, piled up in heaps by sanded-up water or dropping in their tracks from starvation. Again as in the great drought of the sixties, the coyotes, bears and mountain lions pulled the weakened sheep down. In one instance 5000 sheep were killed and fed to hogs. As a last resort many of the ranchers drove their flocks to Arizona, New Mexico or Utah, but the flock loss was enormous. When the rains came again, the sheep pastures remained deserted, as California wool could not command the prices to make it worthwhile to rebuild the flocks. The pastoral period of southern California was over. It was time now for a new character to enter on the scene—the small settler.

CHAPTER 12

"Fruit is abundant, and wine is cheaper than milk"

The new economic pattern of southern California was set a few years after the Civil War with the completion of the Pacific railroad and the systematic subdivision of Abel Stearns' vast landholdings. Stearns, in the fashion of the *Perils of Pauline* of early movie days, had barely been able to hold onto his land after the disastrous drought of the early 1860s. Alfred Robinson, an old friend, approached a number of San Francisco investors with a unique proposal for California—a national promotion and sale of Stearns' holdings to small settlers. Edward F. Northam, Charles E. Polhemus and Sam Brannan were interested. They knew the Pacific railroad would be completed to Sacramento the following year. It was inevitable that a transcontinental road would go through southern California. Already the publicity on the South Coast extolling its real and imaginary virtues had begun to pay off in the first little building boom in Los Angeles and the successful subdivision of Rancho Santa Gertrudes by John G. Downey. Some of the smaller ranchos had buyers as a result of the trail-breaking purchases by the Flints, Bixbys and Irvines. Not the least of the considerations was the fact that Abel Stearns was in no trading position. The cash paid him could be kept to a minimum figure, with the remainder of the payment dependent on property sales. The group formed a company which was popularly known as the Robinson Trust or Stearns Rancho Trust. Under the terms of the agreement signed in May, 1868, Stearns turned over all of his ranchos (with the exception of Rancho Laguna) on the South Coast. For this, Stearns received an eighth interest in the Trust; $1.50 an acre as the parcels were sold; and a cash advance of $50,000 to liquidate his most pressing debts. The agreement involved, according to Robert G. Cleland:

> . . . a total of 177,796 acres, or nearly 178 square miles, and included the following ranchos: Los Coyotes, 48,825 acres; La Habra, 6,698 acres; San Juan Cajon de Santa Ana, 21,572 acres (net); Las Bolsas y Paredes, 33,509 acres (net); La Bolsa Chica, 8,272 acres (net); Jurupa in San Bernardino County, 41,168 acres (net); and La Sierra, in the same county, 17,752 acres. Most of the land was extremely fertile, well adapted to diversified farming, and susceptible of irrigation at moderate cost.[1]

By July of the same year the lands had been surveyed and priced at from five to thirteen dollars an acre. The Los Angeles and San Bernardino Land Company was organized to act as the sales arm of the Robinson Trust. Following the heavy promotional pattern used by the railroads and the canal companies before them, a national and European sales program was launched, supported by brochures and detailed maps. The area was divided into one-mile-square blocks with provision for a road on each side of the block, and the land was to be sold in sections or fractions of sections. The sales terms were one-fourth cash, with the balance to be paid in three years with 10 per cent annual interest on the unpaid balance. The literature and the canned talks of the hired lecturers were flamboyant and certainly conveyed the impression that the climate of southern California was uniformly superb, the soil was perfect for practically all crops, the land was well watered, and new towns were springing up overnight. J. M. Guinn told of his own experience with the persistent sales efforts for the townsite of Savana:

> Just before we cast loose from the wharf at San Francisco a young man came aboard the steamer with an armful of boom literature. . . . These he distributed where he thought they would do the most good. A map and description of the City of Savana fell to my lot. . . . A few weeks later after my arrival in Los Angeles I visited the city. I found it on the western slope of the Coyote Hills, about six miles north of Anaheim. Long rows of white stakes marked the line of streets. A solitary coyote on a round knoll, possibly the site of the prospective city hall, gazed

despondently down the streets upon the debris of a deserted
sheep camp. The other inhabitants of the city of Savana had
not arrived, nor have they to this day put in appearance.[2]

Guinn was right about the land boomer's over optimism in
planning paper cities, but he and many others underestimated
at the time the desperate eagerness for small parcels of cheap
farming land at reasonable interest rates for those days. With
the massive dislocations of the Civil War, particularly in the
South and to a lesser extent in the Border states, the young men
headed west. Huge wagon trains rumbled down through Cajon
Pass, with some of the trains containing a hundred wagons.
Ships arrived at San Pedro loaded with immigrants, many from
Europe. Twenty thousand acres of land were sold in a little
more than a year after the promotional campaign got under way.

Meanwhile, Abel Stearns began fighting with his new partners in the Robinson Trust. As with other Californios, it was
difficult for him to understand that he no longer owned his lands.
He independently leased thousands of acres of Trust land for
sheep pasturage to people like Domingo Bastanchury at ten cents
a head. His partners felt strongly that these leases would hurt
the sale of the land. Even more irritating, Stearns was also
changing established sales terms and conditions on a number of
land sales. The disputes between him and his partners were
progressing beyond the stage of acrimony and approaching the
point of interminable litigation. The issues were resolved in
August of 1871 when Stearns died suddenly at the Grand Hotel
in San Francisco after being in poor health for more than a
year. The body was brought back for burial in Los Angeles in
an 800-pound casket which fell with a crash into the open grave
when the ropes broke. It was a memorable burial for the most
powerful personage on the South Coast for nearly three decades.

Some unknown person made an immaculate personnel decision for the Los Angeles and San Bernardino Land Company.
He hired Robert M. Widney to be the Southern Agent in 1868
and serve as the on-the-spot salesman to sell the Stearns lands

while the national sales promotion got under way. Widney's background was not that unusual for the Americans who went west in the 1850s and 1860s. Leaving home in Ohio at age fifteen, he wandered over the Rocky Mountains area and finally arrived in the goldfields of California. He worked his way through the very new College of Pacific, a Methodist school then at San Jose. He taught mathematics at the college for a bit; studied for and passed the bar; and then headed for the mining camps at Nevada. He was known in the brawling camps as a non-drinker and a dead shot. Still at loose ends at the age of thirty, he heard about the planned subdivision of the Stearns lands and applied for a job with the Trust.

Widney arrived in Los Angeles with his worldly possessions in a trunk and a hundred dollars—a hard-working, intelligent, somewhat humorless man who was to discover he had strong qualities of planning and leadership. The young land agent went to work with the furious but organized energy which was to characterize him for the remaining sixty-three years of his life in Los Angeles. After renting a small office at Main and Arcadia streets, he rode for days over the deserted rolling plains familiarizing himself with the Stearns lands while he listened and talked to the Californios and old settlers. As with all great salesmen and the first of the real California land boomers, he believed in and thoroughly understood the product he was going to sell— the agricultural growth of the South Coast. His enthusiasm, backed by weeks in the saddle and detailed sketches of the land, readily infected the arriving immigrants. Widney would not be the last newcomer to see the South Coast land opportunities which would be missed completely by the old residents. He was convinced that the rolling plains could support huge groves of oranges, lemons and walnuts as well as vineyards. Field crops of alfalfa, barley, cotton and corn would prosper on the deserted range lands that had never been plowed. The climate was favorable, and the land was cheap. Widney prepared circulars and maps which he gave to the new immigrants and mailed throughout the United States and Europe. The persistent problems of cloudy property titles and delays in issuing land patents was a constant problem for the land company selling the Stearns tracts, and Widney found himself becoming an expert land lawyer in addition to his real estate sales work. As his reputation spread, money flowed in from other parts of the country for him to invest in South Coast land. Widney's *Real Estate Advertis*er, which he began printing monthly in 1870, became nationally recognized as the bible on the coastal plains and was the prototype of the best California land-promotion publications.

A serious limitation on the sale and development of the Stearns ranchos was the incredibly bad land transportation. The Southern Pacific promised no relief for years as its railhead crawled leisurely south from San Francisco. There was Banning's "goose pond" at Wilmington miles away, and two landings adjacent to the Stearns properties—Anaheim Landing and Newport Bay.

Two coastal freighters were making weekly stops outside the bar of Alamitos Bay by the late 1860s, as well as lumber schooners and occasional passenger vessels. The cargoes were transferred to eighty-ton lighters which were pulled to the Anaheim wharf on the other side of the bar. Because the ground became marshy during the rainy months, a well-drained dirt road was finally built from the landing to Anaheim. Prior to that, a new trail had to be followed each wagon trip.

Newport Bay as a new small coastal harbor was also used in the Stearns' land company promotions. The Santa Ana River, as with the San Gabriel and the Los Angeles (Porciuncula River on early maps) followed a number of channels over the coastal plain in the most recent geologic period. Prior to 1825, for example, the mouth of the Santa Ana had been at Alamitos Bay while the San Gabriel emptied into the sea at what is now Long Beach. Then, as a result of heavy rains and consequent flooding, the Santa Ana changed its course and emptied into the ocean southeast of the Huntington Beach mesa. When this occurred, a sandy barrier beach or peninsula began to develop in a southeasterly direction, with the river's mouth moving progressively toward the Corona del Mar bluffs and a small sand spit extending from their base. By 1865, when Captain S. S. Dunnells first brought the *Vaquero*, a shallow-draft stern wheeler, across the Santa Ana River bar, the narrow river opening to the sea was about a half mile from the base of the Corona del Mar bluffs. Within Newport Bay, Dunnells found there was a winding and shallow but navigable channel, and he began a regular freight service to Rancho San Joaquin, as well as to some of the Stearns ranchos. Three brothers—John, James and Robert McFadden— built a dock in 1873 about where the present Coast Highway separates the upper and lower Newport bays. This was known as Newport or McFadden's Landing and later Port Orange. In 1876 the McFaddens, with the help of the settlers, dredged a new entrance to the bay next to the Corona del Mar bluffs, the present site of the Newport harbor entrance, a half mile from the natural river mouth. Crossing the bar and coming into the new channel could be an exciting experience in certain kinds of weather and seas, but it was a substantial improvement over the old natural entrance. While far from satisfactory as a port, the shallow bay provided an all-weather harbor along a desolate coast for the new settlers in what is now Orange Country.

The change in course of the Santa Ana River after 1825 had left Abel Stearns a cloudy title on the rich delta area between the Huntington Beach mesa and Bolsa. As a result, this was a natural location for squatters, and they happened to be evangelistic ones at that. While the courts later determined the delta was Stearns Rancho Trust property, in the interim the continued series of revivals and exhortations by camp-riding preachers in the low-lying delta inevitably induced some wag to call the area Gospel Swamp. That was its well-known South Coast name for many years. North of the Gospel Swamp was a temperance colony of Presbyterians where 6500 acres were laid out in forty-acre farms surrounding a 160-acre townsite which the colony called Westminister. This was also part of the rich delta area that grew legendary vegetables in the late 1870s—a 173-pound pumpkin and sweet potatoes each weighing 20 pounds.

California and its gold was known throughout the world. With the availability of rich Stearns lands like Westminister at low prices and the heavy promotional work of the Southern Pacific, the land company and Robert M. Widney himself, southern California began to seem like the magic land of opportunity. The acreage of cultivated land nearly doubled in a two-year period. Euphoric letters of the new settlers began drifting east: "Fruit is abundant, and wine is cheaper than milk."[3] The South Coast found itself in the middle of its first land boom.

CHAPTER 13

"She would pour her dishwater around the young orange trees"

Despite the land-promotion tub-thumping and occasional ecstatic letters home, southern California was no land of milk and honey for the new settlers who came after the Civil War. The advance guard of the California Colony Association found the Riverside area of Rancho Jurupa in the summer of 1870 a dry and very hot wind-swept mesa stretching for miles toward the south, with a growth of brown, baked grass without a tree or shrub. Starting in the fall and running through the winter months, they discovered their desolate mesa was directly in the path of the santana winds rushing down through the Cajon Pass from the Mojave Desert. The high winds swept over the sandy plain "filling all the air with clouds of dust, and seemingly concentrating all their power at the mesa's edge, thundering at our doors day and night, often for three days at a time, as if in rage at our intrusion on their hitherto undisputed territory, as if bent upon the destruction of ourselves and all our effects."[1]

The new settlers in the Riverside area knew nothing about irrigation and little about fruit culture, especially citrus. It was all too evident that windbreaks had to be developed as soon as possible in an area where there were no trees except in the river-bottom lands. But water above all else was the first requirement if anything was to be done with the parched but fertile soil. The Riverside colony decided to build a six-mile canal through its lands from the Santa Ana River. The canal was eight feet wide at the top, six feet on the bottom and three feet deep. Water was carried across small valleys on wooden flumes. Lateral ditches came into the main canal at intervals, with the flow of

water into each ditch controlled by a wooden gate. The basic
canal system was completed in mid-1871 at a cost of $20,000,
twice as much as was originally estimated. The settlers found
their new and expensive canal system was less than satisfactory.
Gophers tunneled through the dirt bank, and the water ran down
and out the gopher holes. Flumes collapsed. Water seepage and
evaporation alone accounted for nearly half the water turned
into the main canal. The owner of a water-storage cistern was a
source of envy to his neighbors. Without a cistern and in the
event of a canal break, which was frequent, there was no water
until the break was repaired, which might take many days. In
the interim a settler without a cistern hauled his water for
household use from the river. When the canal water was available, Robert Hornbeck recalled its flavor and quality:

> The distributing system of the main canal and laterals was
> constantly clogged with weeds and grass. The Indians were
> hired by the company to keep the ditches clean, and to do this
> work they had to get into the main canal with scythes. They
> sometimes wore overalls at this work, but more frequently did
> not, and the spectacle of a gang of Indians, naked except for a
> shirt, wading in the main canal cutting out grass and weeds, was
> too common to excite any notice, even from the people who
> drank the water. . . . It would seem that a water supply drawn
> through an open ditch six miles, which was a regular bathing
> place for children and animals, reeking with decaying vegetation
> and almost boiling under a tropical sun, should have killed us
> all off; but "germs" had not yet been invented, and we were
> in blissful ignorance of the fact that every mouthful of water
> we drank contained microbes enough to kill a regiment. If there
> was a case of typhoid fever in those years, it escaped record.[2]

With water, the first crops and fruit trees were planted at
Riverside. As with other South Coast settlers, in most instances it
was a cut-and-try procedure. Raisin grapes, figs, English walnuts,
olives, peaches, apricots and nectarines were all tried, with vary-
ing degrees of success. The general opinion originally was that
oranges would be mediocre at the best. Even opium poppies
were grown, with some opium being sold to the Chinese laborers. As the acres were planted, eucalyptus seedlings were ob-

tained from Rancho Santa Anita and planted in dense rows for eventual windbreaks. The Australian eucalyptus, which grew rapidly and thoroughly enjoyed the climate, soon became the symbol of the new agriculture on the South Coast. Pepper trees which had been brought to the South Coast from Peru in the days of the missions were extensively planted for shade.

The settlers discovered that the young field plantings and kitchen gardens were eagerly appreciated by the gophers as well as by brigades of rabbits and swarms of grasshoppers. Children were told to shake out their shoes in the morning to dislodge stray scorpions and centipedes. Rattlesnakes and tarantulas gave up ground only grudgingly in the irrigated fields. Coyotes discovered that the kitchen flocks of poultry made very good eating.

After laboriously winning the battle against the gophers and rabbits for the first crops, the Riverside settlers found they had no nearby markets for them. It became routine for a man to load a two-horse wagon and head for Los Angeles, an Inyo mining camp or Fort Yuma over rutted trails in the hope of raising some hard money in his produce. Few settlers were coming in to Riverside, and some were leaving by 1874.

Mrs. Eliza Tibbetts changed the unpromising outlook for the Riverside Colony. Since her friend Mrs. William O. Saunders had gone to all the effort to send her two small orange trees from Washington, D.C., in 1873 she planted them near her kitchen door in Riverside, not only to keep the gophers and rabbits from them but also to water the trees, as her husband, Luther, refused to buy Riverside irrigation water. Eliza soon got into the habit of walking out the kitchen door where she would pour her dishwater around the young orange trees. The citrus liked the climate and Eliza's treatment, and the two trees bore a few oranges in the season of 1876. A number of men who were attempting to grow seedling citrus gathered at the house of George W. Carcelon to examine and test the first navel oranges from Mrs. Tibbetts' citrus tree. The fruit was outstanding, with

only a one-eighth-thick rind and no seeds. Buds from the Tibbetts citrus were successfully transferred to seedling orange trees
by Josiah Cover and Samuel McCoy, and the California orange
industry was born.

Prior to moving out west, the Tibbettses had lived in Washington, D.C. One of their neighbors was William O. Saunders,
who headed a division in the Department of Agriculture which had
been allocated the obscure citrus-fruit specialty. Saunders' wife
and Eliza Tibbetts were good friends, and they corresponded
after Eliza moved to the wilds of southern California. About the
time the Tibbettses left Washington, the United States Consular
Office in Bahia, Brazil, sent several young trees to Saunders'
division. Other trees were budded from them, and a dozen or so
good citrus were the result. This was interesting, but Saunders
knew that the bulk of the farmers of the United States were
geographically in no position to use the experimental trees except perhaps in Florida or southern California. Several of them
went to Florida, with unsatisfactory results. Mrs. Saunders suggested sending two of them to her friend somewhere near the
village of San Bernardino in southern California. Luther Tibbetts picked up those two trees in Los Angeles in December of
1873. Somehow the citrus survived the long trip from the experimental farm in Washington, D.C., as well as the three-day wagon
ride from Los Angeles to Riverside.

Tibbetts had little interest in farming, let alone nursing young
orange trees, and as a result, most of his land remained unculti-
vated. He was "disputatious and eccentric"[3] and was constantly
involved in lawsuits, one of which resulted in his being shot in
the arm. His litigation activities reached the point where they
were very nearly a vocation and ranged from stray stock to water
rights; one of his lawsuits he argued himself before the State
Supreme Court.

Luther Tibbetts had much in common with a breed of new
settlers who were popularly referred to as "Pikes" in the 1870s
on the South Coast. A Pike was described as a man who "often
lives with his family in a wagon; he rarely follows steady industry; he is frequently a squatter on other people's lands; he owns

a rifle, a lot of children and dogs, and if he can read, a law-book. . . . He moves from place to place, as the humor seizes him, and is generally an injury to his neighbors. He will not work regularly; but he has great tenacity of life, and is always ready for a lawsuit."[4] While Luther Tibbetts had many of the characteristics of the true Pike of his day, chance and his wife, Eliza, placed him in a history-making role in the citrus industry.

The Washington Navel Orange, as it was finally called, syn-thesized South Coast agriculture. For the first time its product was clearly the best. This was not mediocre California wool; scrawny range cattle that could only be sold in a Gold Rush atmosphere; or indifferent California wines—but beautiful citrus. Something that would thrive—and sell. By 1880 young and bear-ing orange groves were selling at $1000 per acre. Thirty years after Tibbetts picked up the two little trees in Los Angeles, President Theodore Roosevelt with much ceremony replanted one of those trees in front of the new Mission Inn in Riverside. About that time, over 30,000 carloads of 400 boxes each of oranges were being shipped from the South Coast annually, the Riverside area being the principal shipping point.

By 1874 the Southern Pacific building east from Los Angeles had reached the townsite of Pomona and the railhead at Spadra, twenty-eight miles east of Los Angeles. Stages traveled from the railhead to Riverside three times a week, with a three-dollar fare for a one-way passage. However, it was a wry joke in Riverside during the winter rainy period that these stages came through one week and tried to get back the next. Nevertheless, the railroad seemed practically next door. By the time the one-horse wagons with their railroad-grading crews appeared on the desolate plain north and west of Riverside, they were under minute surveillance by any San Bernardino or Riverside boy who had any gumption at all.

When the Southern Pacific arrived in 1876 at the townsite of Colton, a few miles north of Riverside, it was a cause of cele-bration. The settlers had little interest for a time in the Big Four's railroad monopoly. All they could see was that their fruit, produce and field crops of barley and alfalfa (first called

"Peruvian grass") could move into Los Angeles by rail and thence to San Francisco or by Remi Nadeau's freight wagons to the Inyo mines. Raisins, followed by apricots, were still the prime crop when the railroad arrived, but by the late 1870s it was clear that the one thing to plant was the navel orange. Lemons were marginal because of the cold winters, and limes were completely submarginal for the same reason. Initially, oranges were shipped unwrapped in an ordinary freight car to San Francisco, with the growers selling their fruit for about three cents apiece. With rail transportation and the quality navel orange, along with cheap Chinese labor, which was moving out of railroad construction, the area had all of the ingredients for a major agricultural base.

Ten years after the Civil War, the South Coast was the leading area of the state in the production of grapes and in the manufacture of wines and brandies. The heart of the wine section was around Anaheim and the new towns of Santa Ana and Tustin. Hundreds of thousands of vines had been planted and many small wineries established. Certainly, looking at the sprawling acres of vineyards, Anaheim and the surrounding sections had every reason to expect a prosperous decade in the 1880s. But there was a gnawing matter of concern. Several growers had reported some shriveling of grape leaves on the vine, and the disturbing thing was that the blight seemed to be on the oldest and strongest wine vines. Then the new raisin vines were affected. The season of 1882 showed much more of the blight, and there were more and more worried discussions. A Department of Agriculture expert was called in, with no results. Unfortunately, it was years before the blight was discovered to be a leaf hopper which could be controlled by ladybugs. In the next five years the vineyards were destroyed by the virulent infection, and the farmers were desperate. The prime hope for the Anaheim area was to make the painful seven-year conversion to the booming citrus industry—primarily navel oranges from Riverside plantings. The young groves prospered, and when the time came in 1889 to select a name for the new county (carved out of Los Angeles County) the people called it Orange.

Black powder and picks and shovels were the only tools the Central
Pacific gangs had to drive tunnels through the tough Sierra granite.
A. A. Hart, *courtesy of Society of California Pioneers.*

The heavy framing of Sierra snowsheds, required to support snowdrifts as much as
30 feet in depth, stretched in sections for 40 miles over the mountains. A. A. Hart,
courtesy of Society of California Pioneers.

Leland Stanford. As both a California governor and senator, he kept up the political fences of the Southern Pacific while serving as its president. *Courtesy of Stanford Collections.*

Collis P. Huntington. There was no question in his mind but that he carried the entire burden of the Big Four and the Southern Pacific. *Courtesy of Title Insurance and Trust Company.*

Charles Crocker. A bull of a man with a famous temper, he drove through the construction of the railroad over the High Sierras. *Courtesy of Title Insurance and Trust Company.*

Mark Hopkins. A reticent man, he was noted for his judgment as well as his ability to keep peace among the other strong-minded Big Four members. *Courtesy of Title Insurance and Trust Company.*

Champagne was handed from the funnel-stacked Central Pacific locomotive to the Union Pacific construction crew as the chief engineers shook hands at Promontory Point. A. J. Russell, *courtesy of Oakland Museum.*

Construction started on the inner harbor of San Pedro in 1872 with a breakwater running from Rattlesnake (Terminal) Island to Dead Man's Island in the left background of this 1880 photograph. *Courtesy of Title Insurance and Trust Company.*

Remi Nadeau. He met the challenge of transporting the lead-silver ingots from the Inyo Mountains to Los Angeles. *Courtesy of Security Pacific National Bank.*

Robert M. Widney. The first of the real land-boomers, he early recognized the agricultural potential of the South Coast. *Courtesy of Security Pacific National Bank.*

This tiny 2-2-0 locomotive, the first on the South Coast, was the pride of the Los Angeles and San Pedro Railroad. When the photo was taken, the headlight had not yet been mounted. *Courtesy of Security Pacific National Bank.*

The terminal in Los Angeles of Phineas Banning's San Pedro railroad was opened in 1869 with a wonderful party attended by 2000 people. *Courtesy of Security Pacific National Bank.*

Lumber schooners from the Pacific Northwest began putting into San Pedro routinely with the start of the first Los Angeles boomlet in the late 1860s. *Courtesy of Title Insurance and Trust Company.*

A horsecar of the Spring & Sixth St. R.R. Co. stops at the new three-story Pico House. Built by Pio Pico in 1870, it was Los Angeles' first up-to-date hotel. *Courtesy of Security Pacific National Bank.*

Benjamin D. Wilson. It was his foresight which eventually gave the South Coast a transcontinental railroad and a significant harbor. *Courtesy of Title Insurance and Trust Company.*

F. P. F. Temple. A fine man and a poor banker, his life was ruined with the collapse of the boomlet of the seventies. *Courtesy of Title Insurance and Trust Company.*

Tiburcio Vasquez. The last famous bandido of California, he had a great deal of charisma and substantial Californio support. *Courtesy of Security Pacific National Bank.*

There were far more saloons than churches even when Los Angeles became more respectable, after the seventies. In 1870 the town of 5700 people had over 100 saloons. *Courtesy of Title Insurance and Trust Company.*

Los Angeles' Commercial Street was lined with shops in the early 1870s. Belligerent Joseph Dye was gunned down from the White House Hotel, the two-story building in the right background. *Courtesy of Security Pacific National Bank.*

The Bella Union Hotel had grown to three stories by the early 1870s and was competing with the new Pico House. Even trees had been planted, a sure sign of American influence. *Courtesy of Title Insurance and Trust Company.*

The famous Tehachapi Loop of the Southern Pacific can have the caboose of a long modern freight disappearing into the tunnel as the train's locomotives cross over the tunnel on the skyline above. *Courtesy of Security Pacific National Bank.*

Chinatown had developed in and around Calle de Los Negros by 1871, when the Chinese Massacre occurred in Los Angeles. *Courtesy of Security Pacific National Bank.*

Ygnacio Sepulveda. The son of a famous Californio, he made his own reputation as a courageous judge after the Chinese Massacre in Los Angeles. *Courtesy of Security Pacific National Bank.*

John P. Jones. As a silver-rich Nevada senator, he gave Collis P. Huntington serious worry for a time with his railroad. *Courtesy of Security Pacific National Bank.*

Santa Monica for a time in the mid-1870s was the ocean terminal of John P. Jones' railroad with a 1,740-foot wharf. *Courtesy of Los Angeles County Museum.*

Spring Street in 1885, looking north from First toward the junction of Main and Temple streets, had the first horsecar line in Los Angeles. *Courtesy of Title Insurance and Trust Company.*

Fred Harvey. A chapter of the American West was written when he introduced fine food on the Santa Fe and the Harvey Girls as waitresses at his restaurants. *Courtesy of Santa Fe Railway.*

Arcadia Bandini. First married to Abel Stearns and then to R. S. Baker, she was one of the great personalities of her era in southern California. From *Out West*, Apr. 1909.

The Harvey Girls of the Santa Fe served the famous Fred Harvey food, starting in the 1870s in isolated towns along the railroad. L. W. Eastman, *courtesy of Santa Fe Railway.*

The great railroad rate-war of 1886-87 started the national rush to the South Coast, with the Southern Pacific depositing 120,000 people in Los Angeles in one year. *Courtesy of Title Insurance and Trust Company.*

CHAPTER 14

"Damn me if I want
an interest in
a shooting gallery!"

As in years past, it seemed totally unfair to the South Coast and Los Angeles that northern California and San Francisco would benefit first from gold and then from Nevada silver. Therefore, when Mortimer W. Belshaw in 1868 drove his wagon into Los Angeles with some shiny lead-silver ingots from Inyo County, it was a subject of excited gossip and rumors in every saloon in town. For years prospectors had been picking at the desert mountains in southern California with little result. Yet quantities of silver had been discovered in the West Coast mountain chains in Mexico to the south and Nevada to the north.

The barren Inyo range east of the Sierras and above the marshy Owens Lake and the present town of Lone Pine had been prospected for years. Finally, substantial galena (lead) deposits with associated silver were discovered in 1865 near the top of a mountain at what was called Cerro Gordo. Word began to filter about the Nevada silver camps that there might be a major new silver strike in the Inyo Mountains of California. Belshaw heard the rumors and was interested, since he had spent several years in the Mexican silver mines and related galena-smelting operations. He rode up the steep mountainside to Cerro Gordo from the Owens Valley floor and found an excited group of prospectors who had discovered quartz veins even richer in silver than the original galena discoveries. With his Mexican experience, Belshaw was convinced that the galena deposits were the key to control of Cerro Gordo, as galena was an absolute requirement for smelting the quartz ores for silver. He immediately began the first of a series of moves to gain control of the Union Mine, the heart of the galena structure of Cerro Gordo. For the moment that was the least of his tasks. It was obvious to him that to develop the major silver potential, an expensive eight-mile wagon road must be built from the Owens Valley below up a precipitous and barren mountain to the 10,000-foot elevation level. Then an efficient smelter would have to be constructed on the mining site for a large-scale operation, which obviously meant fuel and water would be serious problems. Further, Belshaw knew the entire operation had to be supported logistically over a tenuous 200-mile trail across deserts and mountains from Los Angeles. All of this meant a substantial amount of mining venture money. He and his partner, Abner B. Elder, found Egbert Johnson of San Francisco, a speculator in silver claims, willing to put up the money, and the United Mining Company was the result. With the funds lined up, Belshaw moved fast.

Building the switchback wagon road up the steep Cerro Gordo grade was a major job. It was done with two-horse wagons, black powder, and pick and shovel work. The road was constructed in three months, and the United Mining Company received its first return on its investment, in September, 1868, by charging a dollar for each two-horse wagon and twenty-five cents for a rider. Meanwhile, Belshaw and Elder had been ordering smelting equipment. As it arrived in San Pedro, it was loaded on wagons for the long trip to the Cerro Gordo for mounting on the newly constructed base of the furnace. In the remarkable time of three months after the opening of the mountain road, the United Mining Company was shipping lead-silver pigs to San Pedro for transshipment to San Francisco. There the silver was refined and sold to the United States Mint.

In a few months, the company was producing well over one hundred lead-silver ingots a day on a seven-day-week basis. Each ingot or pig weighed about eighty-five pounds, with an average value of twenty-five dollars. This was enough to put Cerro Gordo on the map as the beginning of a major silver camp. When Victor Beaudry came on stream with a second smelter in 1870, the Cerro Gordo was turning out nine tons of lead-silver pigs a day, with every indication that the output would increase.

By this time the transportation system in and out of Cerro Gordo was breaking down. Metal ingots were stacked up around the camp, and some of the miners were building the walls of their houses out of them. Food, supplies and equipment, all to be hauled on the long return trip from Los Angeles, were increasingly scarce and expensive. Victor Beaudry knew of Remi Nadeau through his brother, Prudent, who had staked Nadeau in the freight-hauling business a few years earlier. Nadeau had taken on Phineas Banning in the long-haul transportation business and had done so well that he and Banning disliked each other thoroughly. Agreement was reached with Belshaw and Victor Beaudry that Nadeau would handle 130 tons a month of Cerro Gordo ingots, only about half of the current production of the smelters. As time went by, it was clear that Nadeau could do the whole job but only if a major freighting operation with stations along the trail to Los Angeles was set up and staffed. Belshaw and Beaudry agreed to put $150,000 in the freighting company. It was up to Remi Nadeau to solve the overall transportation problems of the Cerro Gordo once and for all.

The wear and tear on Nadeau's men, animals and equipment was enormous as the lead-silver tonnage to be transported from the Cerro Gordo climbed to eighteen tons daily in 1874. The tonnage schedule had to be maintained every day of the year. The temperatures over the trail could easily exceed 120 degrees or be far below freezing; there could be snow on the ground; or desert windstorms could sand up waterholes and make breathing for the men and the teams next to impossible. Yet the bullion trains stolidly moved on the long trail to Los Angeles at two to three miles an hour. The typical rig evolved into a fourteen-mule team (actually twelve mules and two wheel horses) hauling three wooden hulks of wagons with five-foot wheels having six-inch-wide iron rims. The rigs generally traveled in pairs because one could haul the other out of sand or sump holes. Twenty-eight mules were also put on one rig to haul it over San Fernando Pass. The plume of alkali dust of a train could be seen for miles as it crept over the undulating desert wastes. The two-man crew of the following rig were caked and saturated with the burning and penetrating dust.

Coming down the Cerro Gordo grade with eight to ten tons of ingots packed on the floor of the wagons was a thought-provoking experience. The huge wheels were lashed with chain. As a rig skidded down the grade, it might climb up on the first span of animals immediately ahead, maiming or killing them. For this reason, some spare mules were trailed behind the last wagon. Turning a sharp downgrade switchback with the usual drop-off in front was a maneuver which seemed not too involved when it was done correctly. However, unless the maneuver was performed properly, either the result was a fouled-up mess or the rig went over the side of the mountain. Any sensible passenger would prefer by far the Central Pacific Sierra run "down the hill" to Sacramento as compared to going down the Cerro Gordo grade.

Remi Nadeau faced the challenge of his life to keep as many as eighty rigs operating to Cerro Gordo. Somehow he had to provide equipment, men, supplies, water and mule feed. This meant building up an effective organization stretching over an exhausting 200-mile route from Cerro Gordo to Los Angeles, with a headquarters which occupied nearly a square block at Hill and Fourth streets. Although he was a man in his early sixties, Nadeau was in a buckboard or a saddle for days on end checking the staging areas he had set up about fifteen miles apart. In many ways he seemed to be an older Jose Andres Sepulveda and Charles Crocker with a very strong touch of Phineas Banning.

While Nadeau was wrestling with Cerro Gordo transportation, Mortimer Belshaw, Victor Beaudry and several smaller operators had major problems of providing fuel and water for the Inyo mines and supporting camps. Scrub piñion were cut for miles around Cerro Gordo, with smoke signals of the charcoal burners dotting the horizon. As the buildup of Cerro Gordo continued, much more wood was needed. The only source was the steep slopes of the Sierras, miles to the west. In 1873 a

Sierra sawmill was put into operation, with a long flume built to carry the chunks of timber to the Owens Valley floor. The timber was then loaded on wagon trains and taken across the valley and up the Cerro Gordo grade.

Water for the steam boilers and camps was even more of a problem than fuel. There was snow water during the winter months to supplement water packed in by burro from springs several miles away. With water costing as much as fifteen cents a gallon, it was no wonder that Saturday night baths were rarities among the miners. F. P. F. Temple saw a venture-capital opportunity for his new Temple & Workman Bank in Los Angeles. He would provide an adequate supply of water to the Cerro Gordo mines. The idea was simple enough; the execution was not. Ten miles away from Cerro Gordo were some major springs. The water was pumped up 1800 feet to a high ridge and then over extremely rough terrain to Cerro Gordo. The water pipe was put underground to prevent freezing during the winter months. Costs of the project were far higher than anticipated, but in May of 1874 the new pipe line was able to deliver 90,000 gallons of water a day, and the price dropped to four or five cents a gallon.

The miners now had little excuse for not taking weekly baths. There were good reasons they should, for Cerro Gordo met the requirements of a first-rate western mining camp. The girls had arrived from Nevada and San Francisco. Maggie Moore and Lola Travis even had dance floors. Ahead of the girls, of course, had been the highly polished and ornate wooden bars for the saloons and the inevitable green-felt gambling tables. One saloon even had a billiard layout. With the liquor, gambling and women of a roaring silver camp, Cerro Gordo had the accompanying drunken brawls, shootings and murders. As one newcomer muttered to himself after changing his mind about setting up business there: " . . . damn me if I want an interest in a shooting gallery."[1]

While it lasted, Los Angeles loved the Cerro Gordo and hoped for many more like it. When Nadeau's wagons came rumbling down Spring Street with the mule skinner on the rear wheeler snapping his long blacksnake whip at his mules and stray dogs while casually handling a jerk-line through the harness rings as he winked at the pretty girls, it was a first-class sight. His swamper could chew his tobacco and relax from setting the brakes when the wagons rolled down the innumerable arroyos and washes on the trail behind. The rigs delivered the lead-silver pigs to the Commercial Street platform of the railroad depot on Alameda Street. The final stop was the headquarters compound, where the equipment was unharnessed and loading for the return trip got under way, while the mule skinner and the swamper headed for Calle de Los Negros to wash the alkali dust out of their mouths with aguardiente. A small boy in Los Angeles at the time had a hard choice to make as to whether he wanted to be a mule skinner with a fourteen-mule team or an engineer on Phineas Banning's new railroad.

The boy's parents were immersed in the Inyo silver trade, not only the Cerro Gordo but later on the Panamints. There was also a wool boom on, and the horrors of the great drought and smallpox were already fading in Los Angeles' memory. Several hundred tons of lead-silver pigs pouring through the town every month was tangible evidence of the type of prosperity which had pushed San Francisco ahead twenty years before. Support of the burgeoning Inyo trade affected nearly every phase of the South Coast's life. Hay and barley were required in quantity for mule feed. Aguardiente and wine along with beef, mutton, fruits, vegetables and supplies went north on the bullion wagons. Vessels began more regular schedules to San Pedro to supply the machinery, equipment and supplies not available on the South Coast.

Other little California towns, principally Santa Barbara and Visalia in the San Joaquin Valley, had been greedily eyeing the South Coast's silver trade. However, it was San Buenaventura which was the first to nearly upset Los Angeles' bullion carts. Thomas A. Scott planned to bring his Texas Pacific railroad by the southern route to San Diego. As part of his planned development in California, he bought land at the swampy little roadstead port of Hueneme, a few miles from the village around the mission of San Buenaventura, and began construction of a deep-water wharf. With Scott in back of the program, the Ventura County Board of Supervisors in 1871 began making repairs on the wagon trail in the Santa Clara Valley to tie into the Inyo freight trail at what is now Saugus. Ventura had powerful arguments for the Cerro Gordo trade. The difficult route over San Fernando Pass could be eliminated. Probably more important, Hueneme was nearly a hundred miles closer to San Francisco, no small thing for the paddle wheelers and inefficient screw-propeller vessels of the time moving against the prevailing current and swell pattern from the northwest.

The Los Angeles *News* reflected the feelings of Los Angeles at the Ventura threat: "If our city is shorn of the prosperity derived from its present trade monopoly, it will have only the short-sightedness of its own citizens to thank for the disastrous result."[2] The same people who supported Banning's railroad to San Pedro and would support the Southern Pacific a year later organized a Council of Thirty who met at the Bella Union. Agreement was reached that freight rates must be lowered. As a result, the silver trade was held in Los Angeles.

While the Southern Pacific moved slowly south to the townsite of Fresno, it looked again as if the Inyo lead-silver ingots would be permanently diverted northward through Bakersfield. But freight transportation by the Bakersfield entrepreneur backed up badly, with 30,000 ingots waiting for the wagon trains at Cerro Gordo. Remi Nadeau and the mine owners made a deal and the fourteen-mule teams began rolling into Los Angeles again. Nadeau was a hero in the town.

CHAPTER 15

"The unpleasant odor of gas has entirely disappeared since the building of the new sewer"

The stupor which existed on the South Coast with the end of the cattle era began to disappear. Los Angeles was first to feel the effect of the burgeoning Inyo silver trade, the wool boom and the arrival of settlers after the Civil War. Increasingly large numbers of wagon trains creaked down through Cajon Pass. Ships arriving off San Pedro began to carry full passenger loads. Eager and ready to participate in Los Angeles' first boomlet was an interesting assortment of young men who had straggled into the town after the Gold Rush and had already accumulated some money and power.

John G. Downey along with Phineas Banning probably led all the rest of them in drive and imagination. Downey decided in 1865 to subdivide Rancho Santa Gertrudes on which he had foreclosed a mortgage a few years earlier. Never known for his modesty, it was natural that he would call the townsite in the center of the area after himself. The rich land between the Rio Hondo, originally the course of the San Gabriel to the sea, and San Gabriel Rivers sold well and became the prototype of the huge Stearns rancho sales a few years later.

Building construction sharply increased in Los Angeles. The newcomers did not like adobe; they preferred brick and wood. The bricks were made locally, and the demand for lumber signaled the start of a trade with the Pacific Northwest which for years would be a mainstay of San Pedro and help to make Phineas Banning more prosperous. The construction boomlet had reached the point in 1868 where housing was being delayed because of lumber shortages. The new commercial buildings of brick ran north from First Street to beyond the Plaza along Main and Los Angeles streets. The new residential houses were being built as far south as Fourth Street along Fort (Broadway) and Spring streets, as well as along Aliso Street east of Alameda Street.

When Robert M. Widney in the early seventies moved from Spring Street to the present site of the Subway Terminal Building on Hill Street between Fourth and Fifth, he felt that he was locating in the country. As Widney's office was at Main and Arcadia streets, he decided to build a horsecar line from his home into the center of town at the Plaza. With a franchise, he was able to obtain a voluntary assessment of fifty cents a running foot from property owners along the route. Widney started laying ties and tracks on the dirt streets from the new Pico House on Main Street south to Spring where it joined Main and Temple streets. Eventually it passed his house on Hill Street and ended at Sixth and Pearl (Figueroa), where the car shed and stables were built. The town's first car line was single track with bypass switches on Spring and Hill streets for the horsecars to pass each other. The line went into operation in 1874 with a ten-cent fare. Unfortunately, the cars showed a dismaying characteristic of going off the track as they rounded the curves. Widney, never noted for his sense of humor, was disgusted, and the salty comments of the town did not help. He redesigned the track curves himself and shortly thereafter sold the line.

The first horsecar line was only a surface indication of the expansion of the town. Prudent Beaudry saw an opportunity to subdivide the barren and worthless hill property west of the business district. He bought three parcels of property at neglible cost: the steep hillside of New High Street near Sonoratown; twenty acres between Second, Fourth, Charity (Grand) and Hill streets; and another thirty-nine acres between Fourth, Sixth, Pearl (Figueroa) and Charity.

To subdivide successfully, Prudent Beaudry needed water on

his new lands. Beaudry would have been very much of a
gambler indeed to presume he would get his water with the
shaky system which then existed in the town. If the water-
supply dams in the Los Angeles River were not being washed
out with winter rains, the wooden pipes (pine-tree logs with
holes bored in them) were leaking like sieves at the joints. At
the time Beaudry bought his first hill parcel, and probably because of it, the Common Council in 1867 tried again for a town
water supply. It issued $18,000 in water scrip for a water-
collection dam, 5000 feet of iron pipe and, as an afterthought,
a fountain in the grass-grown and littered Plaza. Jean Louis
Sainsevain, a pioneer vintner, took the scrip. He was convinced
that this time he would solve the town's water problem. Sainsevain built a substantial rock dam behind a line of piles in
the Los Angeles River and had a huge forty-foot water wheel
constructed in San Francisco. It was assembled and installed
near the dam in present-day Elysian Park, with the citizens of
the town being impressed as much by Sainsevain's wheel as by
his energy and optimism. The plan was to turn the water into
a flume from the dam and present it to the water wheel, which
would raise it thirty-six feet to a reservoir zanja. From the
reservoir the major zanja, or Zanja Madre, would distribute the
water to its tributaries. The planning was sound; then the next
heavy winter storm took out the dam. As usual, Los Angeles was
back to its water-cart peddlers.

Prudent Beaudry convinced John S. Griffin and Solomon
Lazard, two other born entrepreneurs, to join him in the purchase of the project from Sainsevain, who definitely wanted out
of his water contract with the town. This they did, repairing
and strengthening the dam and laying iron pipes. Meanwhile,
Beaudry was hedging his bets on water for his speculative hill
property. The Canal and Reservoir Company with his aggressive
financial support was organized in 1868, the same year in which
he and his two partners established the Los Angeles Water
Company to take over Jean Sainsevain's contract with the town.
The idea of the Canal and Water Reservoir Company was to

build a twenty-foot dam a little below the present site of Echo Park and construct a zanja down Arroye de Los Reyes to Beaudry's hill district. As part of the deal with the town, some of the remaining pueblo lands were turned over to the Canal and Reservoir Company as a subsidy. As a further fail-safe on the near term for an assured water supply for his planned subdivision on the Temple Street hills, Prudent Beaudry decided to pump water from the old Abila springs into two reservoirs near where Sunset Boulevard now terminates. The reservoir water would then be pumped up some 250 feet and carried through pipes to his hill properties.

After a heated controversy, the Common Council gave Beaudry's Los Angeles Water Company a thirty-year water franchise for the town. While these arguments were going on, the Echo Park dam and zanja were built along with Beaudry's Abila Springs project. The Common Council in an unusual burst of advanced planning also authorized the investigation of another reservoir further west which later was known as the Silver Lake Reservoir. By mid-1869, Prudent Beaudry had water on his hill property and began to auction off the subdivided lots. Harris Newmark, who was no friend of his, estimated the subdivider cleared $30,000 on the twenty-acre parcel and $50,000 on the thirty-nine-acre property. In a four-year period after 1868, some 2000 homes were built in Los Angeles, a marked change from the lethargic pace of the town of a few years before. The completion of Banning's little railroad to Wilmington was a major factor in supporting this construction boomlet.

Phineas Banning liked mechanical gadgets. Shortly before the Civil War he bought a steam wagon which reputedly would move at five miles an hour. Weeks before the arrival of the contraption by ship at his dock, Banning was telling his friends how he would arrive majestically in Los Angeles on his vehicle with Banning, of course, at the tiller. The epitaph of the episode was sadly reported by the Los Angeles *Star*: "The steam-wagon is at San Pedro, and we regret to learn that it is likely to remain there. So far, all attempts to reach this city with freight have failed."[1]

It was inevitable that Banning would lead all the rest in his railroad enthusiasm. He was determined to have one, and he knew where he would run it—from his dock in the "goose pond" at Wilmington to Los Angeles twenty-one miles away. But there were problems. It required a good deal of money. He needed a state charter and a large local-government subsidy. The first part was easy; the second was not. He managed to get himself elected to the state senate and forthwith began his usual effective lobbying work for the state charter, which he speedily obtained in 1865. Banning then found that his political fences had come apart in Los Angeles while he had been lobbying in Sacramento. His archrival for years in harbor freighting, J. L. Tomlinson, was not about to let Banning have his railroad. State charter or not, it was clear that there would be no local subsidy at the time.

But Banning had the railroad fever and bulldog determination. Further, he didn't like Tomlinson. In 1868, with his state charter in hand for the Los Angeles and San Pedro Railroad and his local political fences presumably mended, he proposed Los Angeles vote $225,000 of bonds of a maximum financing total of $500,000. This time he expected strong opposition, and he got it. Banning and his friends argued the proposed Southern Pacific Railroad would come to Los Angeles on the southern transcontinental route if there was a line to San Pedro. The opposition's arguments ranged from the creation of an intolerable tax burden to a port monopoly for Banning and his friends. The local subsidy was approved by the razor-thin margin of thirty-nine votes, with the usual and realistic remarks that the Banning crowd had more money to spend buying votes than the opposition.

Banning now began to enjoy himself. As usual, he was indefatigable. At any hour he could be counted on to appear at the shop in Wilmington which had been set up to build the wooden freight and passenger cars with the beautiful legend

"L.A. & S.P.R.R." carefully painted on the sides. His booming voice was constantly heard directing the scrapers and horse carts on the roadbed as the railroad moved toward Los Angeles on what is now Alameda Street. Probably the best day of all was in January, 1869, when he swung aboard a light-draft schooner moored alongside his dock. A tiny 2-2-0 locomotive was unloaded from the ship and ceremoniously christened the *San Gabriel.* In a few days, oftentimes with Banning at the throttle, the *San Gabriel* was hauling flatcars of ties and rails. Meanwhile construction had begun on a depot at the southwest corner of Commercial and Alameda streets in Los Angeles. By summer, the distant whistle of the *San Gabriel* could be heard in the Plaza, and September 7, 1869, the last rails were spiked in. At last Los Angeles had a railroad, even if it was only twenty-one miles long.

Parts for a 4-4-0 locomotive, medium size for its day, had arrived at Wilmington. The manufacturer had misspelled its name "Los Angel*os*" on the tender, but there was no time to correct it, for Banning had invited all of Los Angeles to take a free round-trip ride to Wilmington and then attend a grand ball at the new town depot. About two thousand people took him up on his offer, and the party went on "until an advanced hour of the morning."[2] There was a massive set of hangovers evident around town the next business day.

The little railroad was a financial success from its inception, as both the silver and the wool trade were beginning to peak and immigrants were arriving daily. The area about the depot was crowded with the silver-lead freight teams from the Inyo mines along with the drays and light wagons loaded with wool, merchandise and feed. The passenger fare to the harbor was $2.50. Steamer days made for a major traffic jam on Alameda and Commercial streets around the depot. Along with the passengers and their friends were the touts for the hotels, gambling houses, saloons and whorehouses. The conversation shifted from Spanish to English in midsentence, as the town was now bilingual. Street vendors hawked their fruit, peanuts, tortillas and expensive iced lemonade, as well as chicken and tough shredded beef cooked on charcoal broilers. The drunks rolled out of the nearby saloons, and at least one of the dozen-man police department wearing his standard slouch hat was on duty.

If for no other reason, the policeman was there to pick up the lads who were leaving Los Angeles without paying their bills, legal or otherwise. Los Angeles was still a very tough little town in the seventies. To add to the confusion and the usual number of runaway horses, it required only a minor fire in the district to have the two competing fire companies arrive in the depot area, with the following pack of yapping and biting mongrel dogs. If the weather was hot, a steamer day at Mr. Banning's station had much in common with the daily train arrival in an isolated Mexican town near a flourishing mining area a century later. There was all the excitement, reek of cooking and horse manure along with the smell of sweat. Phineas Banning thoroughly enjoyed his little railroad. On top of that, he and his friends made money out of it.

There were no bridges across the Los Angeles River until 1870. Prior to that time the river was usually forded at Aliso Street. During heavy winter rains when the riverbed swelled to flood levels, the ford was impassable, and Los Angeles was isolated. Between the river and the small bluffs (later called Boyle Heights) on the east side of the river was a fertile strip of bottom land with water which had been planted for both wine and table grapes with cuttings from San Gabriel. The Old Mission Vineyard, as it was called, was bought in 1858 for $3000 by Andrew A. Boyle, an Irishman who came to Texas as a boy with his family in the 1830s. Like so many others, he followed the Gold Rush as a merchant to California and finally ended up in Los Angeles. Boyle also bought the bluff area (later to be named after him) above the vineyard at twenty-five cents an acre at public auction. His friends thought that figure was too high, as, with no water, the land was considered worthless. Boyle built a brick house on the barren bluffs and planted pepper trees. Water was hauled up for house and garden by hand. This type of feverish planting and laborious irrigation of young trees around their houses by the Americans was always incomprehensible to most of the Californios.

The lands immediately east of Boyle Heights had only limited water for sheep-grazing all year around and was also original pueblo land. Dr. John S. Griffin along with Hancock M. Johnston bought 2000 acres from the town for fifty cents an acre in 1863. This was later developed by Griffin and Johnston as East Los Angeles. The same year Boyle acquired his vine-yard, Dr. Griffin, who was engaged in many other activities besides medicine, bought Rancho San Pasqual where Pasadena is now located. With the flurry of activity and building ex-pansion in Los Angeles after the Civil War, Boyle, Boyle's son-in-law, William H. Workman, and Griffin began lobbying at local and state levels for a bridge across the Los Angeles River. The river varied from a small stream of water in September wandering desultorily over a wide sandy bed packed with large stones, to a raging torrent of water in the winter months, rolling the same stones along the bottom and crazily spinning tree trunks in the current. Finally, the state agreed to put up the money for a covered bridge lighted with kerosene lamps at Macy Street. It seemed unusual to the citizens of the town that the state would design a covered bridge in a land where there was no snowfall and which had rain only a portion of the year. At any event, the bridge was completed in 1870 and in the next fifteen years uncovered bridges were built at Downey Avenue and Main, Aliso, First, Seventh and Ninth streets. The original covered bridge was the only one of the early bridges which stayed in commission throughout all of the winter storms, as the Aliso and First Street approaches were usually washed out. In one such storm two horses trapped on the First Street bridge structure were watered and fed by boat rowed through the strong currents and spinning debris.

With the river bridged, it was inevitable that pressure would start for city water east of the river as well as system improve-ments in the central town itself. Completed in the late seventies, a 3600-foot tunnel was built, paralleling the new Southern

Pacific track, to springs in the Elysian Hills for a second source of water. The old Zanja Madre was lined with concrete for 8000 feet to Aliso Street, and zanjas from a reservoir near Macy Street and Mission Road were built east of the river. With water, a heavy subdivision program in Boyle Heights and East Los Angeles got under way.

Los Angeles worried about its water supply but gave little thought to its sewers for many years. The Bella Union Hotel built a small wooden sewer in the fifties to connect with the nearest zanja below Los Angeles Street. When periodically the sewer burst, the tenants of the Mellus Block next to the sewer complained bitterly. When Francis Mellus plugged the sewer up, there would be equally strong outbursts from the guests at the Bella Union. The first town sewer was built in 1873 of brick and wood, and the sewer system gradually expanded from that time. The new Pico House was able to advertise proudly in 1874 that "the unpleasant odor of gas had entirely disappeared since the building of the new sewer."[3]

Hotel and rooming-house space during Los Angeles' first boomlet was expensive and scarce to nonexistent. The Bella Union added another story. When Pio Pico started building his hotel in 1870, the first three-story structure in town across from the Plaza on Main Street, the other three hotels—the Bella Union (shortly to be called the St. Charles), the Lafayette and the United States—began to modernize. After all, the Pico House was going to have bathrooms for both sexes on each floor. Ten years after the Pico House was built, the Natick House was erected at First and Main streets at a cost of $125,000. But Remi Nadeau topped everything in 1882. His friend Harris Newmark told him he was crazy when he paid $20,000 for a hotel site at First and Spring streets. The Nadeau Hotel was four stories and the tallest building in town. It had the town's first elevator—considered by the citizens to be a major indication of modern progress. The Nadeau was a financial success from the day it opened.

Part of the modernization of the older hotels with the town's expansion was the installation of gas for lighting. The first gas plant using imported coal was built in 1865 and located on New High Street. The price was very high, initially ten dollars a thousand cubic feet. After loud protest over the rates the price dropped to six dollars by the time the first gas street lights were installed on Main Street in 1876. Even so, most of the homes were still using coal-oil (kerosene) lamps at the time because of the cost of the fuel and piping installation.

By the mid-sixties coal-oil lamps were rapidly replacing the smelly tallow candles for lighting on the South Coast. At sixty-five cents a gallon, coal oil was not cheap and was imported through San Francisco from Pennsylvania. There was little question that there was petroleum (from which coal oil was made by a primitive distillation process) on the South Coast. In many places it could be seen and smelled as it oozed to the surface of the land and water. During the eighties, when Santa Barbara was first being promoted as a health resort, the local doctors solemnly asserted that "the oleaginous fumes wafted ashore by the prevailing winds were an effective panacea for respiratory diseases."[4] A small promontory on the present University of California, Santa Barbara, campus was known for years as Coal Oil Point. Probably the first attempt at drilling an oil well on the South Coast was made by Major Max von Stroble on Rancho Brea in 1865. Shortly thereafter Phineas Banning, with a retinue of familiar names as officers and directors, including Downey, Charles L. Ducommum, Griffin, Wilson, Dr. J. B. Winston, Matthew Keller and Volney E. Howard, formed the Pioneer Oil Company to drill for oil on Griffin's Rancho San Pasqual and other locations, such as Rancho Camulos near Newhall. None of the drilling ventures was successful. The Pennsylvania cable-tool rigs of the day could not quite go even to the relatively shallow depths of the oil pools in southern California.

The South Coast has never had to defer to any other area in the world in the stickiness and wetness of its adobe clay mud during the rainy months and the adobe's cast-iron hardness during the dry period, which can still cast off a penetrating and irritating dust. Los Angeles had no paved streets until 1887, when first Main and then Spring and Fort streets were paved.

If possible, during the first boomlet after the Civil War, the dirt streets during the rainy months were worse than before. The heavy wagon wheels churned the black gummy mud to the consistency of well-thickened oatmeal, with about the same holding power; and some of the wooden and brick sidewalks teetered into this soupy mass of the street. It was no wonder that horsecar transportation was popular, even though the cars were constantly getting stuck in the mud during the winter months.

Mud or not, Los Angeles was proud of itself by the early seventies. In a period of five years the town had nearly doubled in size to a population of 9000 and the days of the "full pockets" were back again. All that the boosters and land boomers felt was needed to fulfill the town's and the South Coast's new manifest destiny was a direct tie-in with a transcontinental railroad.

CHAPTER 16

"The iron horse poked his nose through the San Fernando Tunnel this evening at six o'clock"

Transportation of the South Coast's products was the key to its future economic development after the Civil War. Cloudy property titles were important restraints but secondary to the area's enormous isolation. There were no real natural harbors. The railroads were inevitable, but when? And even when they arrived, it was possible that the South Coast would only be tapped by a casual branch line.

The man who saw all of this most clearly was Benjamin D. Wilson. His qualifications as a Californio were impeccable, and he was well liked and respected throughout the state. After the completion of the Pacific railroad, there were strong feelings in California that a railroad subsidy of 5 per cent of a county's assessed valuation was no longer required to encourage railroad construction. Wilson disagreed, and led the successful fight in the state legislature to retain the subsidy provision for Los Angeles and seven other counties. Then, at his own expense, he went to Washington to lobby for the southern transcontinental route through Los Angeles. The national railroad legislation was passed in early 1871, including the Los Angeles proviso. Equally important to the South Coast, Wilson was able to lobby through the same session of Congress a $200,000 initial appropriation for the development of an inner harbor at San Pedro.

Meanwhile, the Southern Pacific had continued its slow crawl down the San Joaquin Valley. The railroad bypassed in 1872 what Collis P. Huntington considered to be an insolent Visalia

because the valley town refused to grant a subsidy to the
Southern Pacific. Benjamin Wilson told the South Coast people
that they had better make a deal with the Southern Pacific, as
the Big Four might have ample power in the Congress to have
the key phrase "by the way of Los Angeles" eliminated from the
railroad act. By heading directly from the Tehachapis to Fort
Yuma and bypassing Los Angeles, the Southern Pacific could
eliminate fifty miles of railroad, and more important, save the
heavy expense of tunneling under the San Fernando Pass in the
Santa Susana Mountains. Wilson received the needed support
on the South Coast. After a mass meeting, a steering committee
met, and a conference was arranged with the Big Four in San
Francisco. John G. Downey and Harris Newmark met with
Collis P. Huntington at his headquarters at the Grand Hotel in
the spring of 1872. After a month of intermittent negotiations in
which Wilson was involved, the Los Angeles committee reluctantly accepted the hard and arrogant trading of the Big Four.
It was a $602,000 package consisting of county bonds in the
amount of 5 per cent of the assessed property valuation and
the $225,000 city and county investment in the successful San
Pedro railroad which Phineas Banning had built three years
before. In return, among other things the Southern Pacific agreed
to build a minimum of fifty miles of main trunkline through Los
Angeles County and a branch line to Anaheim within fifteen
months after bond-ballot approval.

The pro-railroad forces on the South Coast knew they would
have a hornets' nest of opposition on the terms which had been
negotiated and which required a vote of the county and the little
town. Further, anti-Southern Pacific sentiment was beginning to
build up. Two relative newcomers led the pro-railroad forces—
Robert M. Widney, the land agent for the Stearns Rancho Trust,
and Harvey K. S. O'Melveny, a lawyer and president of the Los
Angeles Common Council. The opposition was headed by Benjamin Peel, who wrote in the Los Angeles *News*: "I can call to
mind a score, yes, fifty towns that gave large subsidies to have
a railroad run through them, that were literally gutted by the
road."[1]

As the November 5, 1872, election date approached for the approval of the Southern Pacific subsidy, Robert M. Widney wrote and mailed a fourteen-page pamphlet to every voter in the county giving the reasons for subsidy approval. It was an effective and well-timed document, particularly as the Texas Pacific was offering to come up to Los Angeles from its proposed terminal in San Diego and asking only for the county subsidy, not the San Pedro railroad. On the day before the Southern Pacific bond election, there was the usual buying of votes, with the Southern Pacific forces being better heeled and cleverer. It was not really necessary, as the measure won decisively. The bond subsidy was the first major concession by the South Coast to the Big Four but not the last by any means.

While none of the lines went any distance, Los Angeles was beginning to look upon itself as a rail center in 1874. The new Southern Pacific tracks north followed the west bank of the Los Angeles River near what is now Elysian Park and then crossed the river and terminated at San Fernando Mission, six miles from the San Fernando Pass. The railhead to the east was at the townsite of Spadra, twenty-eight miles away. The Anaheim branch line had been completed as far as the village of Downey from the Florence station of the San Pedro railroad. And the rich Nevada senator, John P. Jones, had incurred the wrath of Collis P. Huntington by beginning the construction of a railroad from a new port of Santa Monica to Los Angeles.

San Pedro had long been the central port for Los Angeles and the South Coast. With Banning's new railroad and the new Dead Man's Island breakwater, the port's position seemed secure for the Southern Pacific and its San Pedro railroad. Silver millionaire John P. Jones had other ideas because of his extensive mining operations in Inyo's Panamint Mountains. He wanted his own rail transportation from the mines to his own ocean terminal, with an eventual rail tie-in with the Union Pacific and possibly the proposed Texas Pacific to San Diego.

Jones bought two-thirds of Rancho San Vicente from its

recent purchaser, Colonel R. S. Baker, in 1874, and the two of them began the promotion of the new town of Santa Monica. Jones moved aggressively on his plans. Construction was pushed on a railroad to Los Angeles from a 1740-foot Santa Monica wharf also under construction. A heavy promotional program was launched for Santa Monica using such alliterative phrases as "The Zenith City by the Sunset Sea." Auction sale of Santa Monica lots began in July of 1875, and the railroad to Los Angeles was operating the following December. Several cuts above the Southern Pacific terminal on Alameda Street, the Los Angeles depot of Jones' road was an impressive structure, with two towers on San Pedro Street near Fourth Street. Within a year Santa Monica had a population of a thousand and was boasting loudly that several hundred vessels, including the largest ships of the Pacific Mail Steamship Company, had already loaded or discharged at the port in all weathers. Viewing the money and furious energy of John P. Jones, the Southern Pacific and Los Angeles began to take considerably more than a casual interest in the "Zenith City by the Sunset Sea" and Senator Jones' railroad plans.

Jones called his line the Los Angeles and Independence Railroad. He made it clear that he intended to build his road through Cajon Pass to the high desert and from there to the Inyo mining areas. It would be logical then to tie in with the Union Pacific. The South Coast and Inyo County thought the plan was wonderful and supported it heavily with stock subscriptions. The Southern Pacific emphatically did not. Not only would Jones' plans give the Union Pacific a tremendous bargaining advantage on transcontinental traffic, but equally as important, the proposed Los Angeles and Independence tracks would be a barrier to the Big Four's plans of establishing a transcontinental road via the southern route. Cajon Pass was the first prize, and the Southern Pacific lost it decisively.

James U. Crawford, Jones' engineer, surveyed and staked the key pass. He was able to bring in laborers in the fall of 1874 and had the forethought to build winter quarters in the Cajon. The competing Southern Pacific engineers arrived in the pass

at about the same time as the winter rains and snows. Jones'
men were prepared for a rugged winter; the Big Four's people
were not, and they retreated to the San Bernardino Valley. By
spring of 1875, the Los Angeles and Independence Railroad had
clearly won Cajon Pass.

Meanwhile, Collis P. Huntington began to pull his Washington strings for a route amendment to strike the "by the way
of Los Angeles" proviso from the railroad legislation of 1871,
the very thing which B. D. Wilson had feared. This was stopped
by effective and organized South Coast resistance. Huntington
also instructed William Hood to begin building on a crash
basis from the Tehachapis direct to Fort Yuma. This maneuver
would effectively fence in the Los Angeles and Independence
Railroad when it emerged into the high desert at Cajon Pass
from moving north to the Inyo mining areas and an eventual
hookup with the Union Pacific. It also meant, of course, that in
effect Los Angeles and the South Coast would only be on the
branch line of the Southern Pacific. Los Angeles, San Bernardino
and Inyo County united in raising money for Senator Jones'
road. "Carry the narrow gauge through the Cajon Pass at a
gallop"[2] became the battle cry.

Huntington, however, had luck running on his side. By the
late summer of 1876, Jones had 300 feet of an 1800-foot key
tunnel completed in the Cajon, the last major obstacle before
the line could break out into the high desert. Everything changed
shortly thereafter. Nevada silver speculation collapsed with a
roar. Virginia City burnt to the ground. Senator Jones was in
the process of losing one of the several fortunes he was to earn.
Huntington forthwith made an offer to him for the Los Angeles
and Independence—$100,000 in cash, a $25,000 note and $70,000
in Southern Pacific bonds. Jones finally took the offer in May of
1877. As the San Fernando Tunnel had been completed the
previous year, the Southern Pacific stopped all of the work in
the Cajon. Jones' wharf at Santa Monica was partially dis-
mantled, and rate charges on both the Santa Monica and the
San Pedro lines were increased sharply by the Big Four. Santa
Monica, the Zenith City by the Sunset Sea, shrank to a village of

several hundred people. The elephant memory of the Big Four would not forget the South Coast's enthusiasm and financial support of Senator Jones and his railroad.

The Big Four had an expensive decision to make even before the serious threat of Senator Jones' railroad was eliminated. The Southern Pacific's efforts to have the proviso "by the way of Los Angeles" struck from the railroad act of 1871 had not been successful. Further, the $602,000 subsidy package voted by Los Angeles would be forfeit if the San Francisco-Los Angeles connection was not completed by November 5, 1876. On the other hand, engineering estimates for driving a 7000-foot tunnel through San Fernando Mountain were high, and there was engineering concern as to unknown rock structures which could force costs even higher.

Finally, in early March, 1875, Collis P. Huntington made the decision in New York after his other three partners agreed. William Hood, assistant chief engineer who had directed the Tehachapi construction, was told to build the San Fernando, to be one of the longest tunnels at that time in the world. Hood called in his key tunnel superintendent, Frank Frates, and gave him the difficult assignment. The first powder blast for a deep 500-foot cut near the present town of Newhall was set off on March 22, 1875. Sixteen months and $2,000,000 later, the two ends of the San Fernando Tunnel joined in the heart of the mountain.

The tunnel project was a herculean engineering and construction job. Frank Frates found the rock structure of the mountain to be heavily fissured, with the fissures filled with a sticky blue clay and holding a heavy accumulation of underground water and even some oil. Frates received his first bitter taste of what was ahead when he was forced to abandon his tunnel opening in the northern face because of constant cave-ins and go deeper down into the side of the mountain. It was evident to Frates and William Hood that they were involved in a tunnel engineering problem far different and more serious than anything they had experienced in the Sierras and the Tehachapis. Frates asked for and got a sharply increased tunnel budget. Requisitions were placed for a large number of steam-driven pumps to attempt to control the underground water. Heavy timber specifications were upgraded, and sharply increased timber usage was planned. The decision was made to sink three shafts from the surface of the mountain so work could go on day and night at eight faces of the tunnel. But above all else Frates now knew he needed much more manpower than planned, with the men working under nearly intolerable conditions by the light of tallow candles. Only the Southern Pacific of the time with its vast mountain experience could have provided Frates the experienced foremen, the carpenters, and above all else, the Chinese labor which he required.

The tunnel work force by the beginning of 1876 had grown to 1500 men, most of them Chinese, supported by hundreds of teamsters, storekeepers, blacksmiths and cooks working from the railhead at the village of San Fernando, six miles away, to the camps strung across the top of the mountain.

But Frank Frates and William Hood had still underestimated the costs and time necessary to conquer the San Fernando. Reports of survey teams to the San Francisco headquarters of the Southern Pacific were increasingly pessimistic as to whether the tunnel would ever be completed with the problems being encountered. The continued cave-ins, the underground water, the clay, and the air in the tunnel workings which was so humid and bad that " . . . the candles disposed along the sides of the tunnel burn but dimly"[3] were generating increasing lassitude and fear even in the veteran workers. However, the indomitable and trained crews persisted. The southern face of the tunnel reached a half mile deep into the mountain by April of 1876, and the rest of the tunnel was moving ahead at the rate of twenty-four feet a day.

Hood could finally give the eagerly awaited word to the construction gangs in the Tehachapis—start laying tracks across the desert to the northern face of the tunnel. On August 12, 1876, a memorable message clicked off the telegraph in Los Angeles:

"The iron horse poked his nose through the San Fernando Tunnel this evening at six o'clock and neighed long and loud his greeting to the citizens of Santa Clara Valley."[4] As the good news spread through the town, the noise in Buffum's Saloon on Spring Street reached a crescendo. The cannon in front of Wood's Opera House (the recently renamed Merced Theater) was fired repeatedly as an impromptu torchlight parade got under way.

Charles Crocker, president of the Southern Pacific at the time, drove a golden spike on the new roadbed near the mouth of Mint Canyon on September 5, 1876, and Los Angeles was officially connected by railroad to San Francisco. The spike-driving ceremony was anti-climatic after the conquering of the San Fernando, although an elaborate celebration was staged in Los Angeles, including "a banquet, a ball, and illuminations"[5] accompanied by the incessant booming of the opera house cannon. Probably the most memorable aspect of the meeting of the railheads was the spectacle of hundreds of Chinese, spaced along the track, standing at attention while holding their long shovels as the official train went by. But to the average citizen in Los Angeles, the arrival of the private cars of Charles Crocker and Leland Stanford was of most interest. The cars had come all the way from San Francisco on the new road, and this was solid evidence that Los Angeles and the South Coast were finally part of a transcontinental railroad system.

Southern Pacific trains came into Los Angeles on a scheduled basis late in 1876. The Big Four of course were interested in adding another fiefdom such as the South Coast to their empire, while their forces were engaged in warfare with the likes of the Los Angeles and Independence Railroad. Prominent South Coast men like Harris Newmark did not understand that they were now vassals to the Big Four. They would learn. When Leland Stanford came to see Newmark some months after the opening of the Southern Pacific to Los Angeles, he fatuously told Stanford " . . . that our relations with the steamship company had always been very pleasant, but that we would be very

glad to give his line a share of our business, if rates were satisfactory."[6] Shortly after Newmark's conversation with Stanford,
the Southern Pacific announced the freight rates on its Los
Angeles to San Pedro railroad would be increased from eight
to as high as thirty dollars a ton. As the largest Los Angeles
shipper, Newmark decided to fight the Southern Pacific. Along
with several other merchants he took a three-year charter on
James McFadden's steamship *Newport* and proposed to bypass
the Southern Pacific completely.

The merchant group were educated to their vassal status
rapidly and expensively. The railroad posted a rate schedule of
three dollars a ton between San Francisco and way stations north
of Los Angeles and carried some heavy items free of charge
from Los Angeles to San Francisco. Harris Newmark and his
associates realized that they were being left to die on the vine,
and it would not take long. Phineas Banning, who now was part
of the Southern Pacific organization, was humbly asked to inter-
cede with the Big Four. Leland Stanford's reply to the peace
feeler was enough to strike terror into the hearts of the new
vassals: "The Railroad Company rather than make a single
concession would lose a million dollars in the conflict."[7] The
Big Four's terms were unconditional surrender, and that was
what it got from the Newmark group.

Newmark had received his painful education. He happened
to be first of a long line of growers and merchants to be broken
to the harness. The usual practice was mailed-fist pricing to the
maximum of what the traffic would bear. If a shipper was sending carloads of potatoes to San Francisco, the freight agent expected to be told accurately how much the potatoes had cost
the shipper and what he expected to sell them for. The difference
would be the railroad freight costs and, if all went well, a small
profit for the shipper. If it did not go as planned, the shipper
lost money. Shippers learned by bitter experience to provide
accurate cost and selling prices to the monopoly or their produce
would rot in the fields.

Early in the transportation monopoly development in southern
California, Charles Crocker, one of the Big Four and president

of the Southern Pacific at the time, visited his South Coast fiefdom in September of 1877. He was asked to confer with the Los Angeles Common Council in a public meeting after there had been a large mass demonstration at Union Hall against the Southern Pacific's rate practices. Crocker, a bull of a man and not one noted for his patience or deviousness, agreed to meet with the Council. The chambers of the Common Council consisted of one small, dark room with a rough wood floor stained by tobacco juice. When Crocker arrived, he found the room jammed with people and thick with heavy cigar smoke and the smell of sweat. Crocker stood for an hour while routine town business was conducted. Finally, he made a short statesman-like speech in which he said that the railroad had invested a great deal of money in coming to the South Coast, and it was necessary to realize proper interest on its investment. When he was done, one of the spectators, Isaac W. Lord, asked permission to tell a little story. Lord then told about a man who spent $150,000 to build a hotel in the middle of the desert. The new hotel sat vacant for months until finally a solitary guest stayed overnight. On checking out the next morning, the departing guest was presented with a bill for $75. On his demanding an explanation, the hotel owner told him that the hotel had cost $150,000 and therefore he, as the first and only guest, should obviously pay his part of the interest on the investment.

Lord's little fable was greeted with howls of appreciative laughter from the packed crowd. Prodding questions started coming at Charles Crocker from all sides until finally, after being reminded of the large railroad subsidy voted by the South Coast, the famous Crocker temper went off with a bang:

"I wish to God you had your bonds back and we had our rails taken up. It would have been millions of dollars in our pockets if, instead of coming out of our way down here, we had taken the Mojave cut-off and gone back of those mountains yonder to the Colorado.[8]

"If this be the spirit in which Los Angeles proposes to deal with the railroad upon which the town's very vitality must depend, I will make grass grow in the streets of your city!"[9]

With this remark, Charles Crocker stalked out of the meeting, and left Los Angeles shortly thereafter. His threat very nearly became an actuality for Los Angeles and the South Coast during the next several years.

Fort Yuma at the Colorado River continued to be Collis P. Huntington's objective, after he had brushed aside the Cajon Pass threat of Jones' Los Angeles and Independence Railroad. The veteran construction crews of the Southern Pacific moved east out of Los Angeles toward San Gorgonio Pass, the lower deserts and the Colorado River, while a spur line was completed to Anaheim from the Florence Station of the San Pedro line. San Bernardino was punished for its independence, with the line passing a few miles south and through a new townsite called Colton, named for David D. Colton, a close associate of the Big Four. The west bank of the Colorado River was reached in May of 1877, which theoretically was as far as the Southern Pacific could go without Federal Government concurrence. The Texas Pacific, still 1200 miles away, thought it had already been given general approval to build through the large Indian reservation on the east bank of the Colorado across from the Southern Pacific railhead. Each road began pressuring the War Department for permission to build through the reservation immediately. After much vacillation the authorization was refused to both of them. Stories vary as to how the next episode was allowed to occur; the fact was that in a week's time the Southern Pacific threw a wooden cantilever bridge across the Colorado River to the reservation, and the Yuma military garrison did not stop the work. A month later, work trains rolled into Fort Yuma. By October of 1877, Huntington had a presidential executive order which enabled him to begin building through Arizona and New Mexico territories, and he was working closely with Thomas Peirce, whose railhead was at San Antonio, Texas, with his Galveston, Harrisburg and San Antonio Railroad.

The Southern Pacific reached the old walled town of Tucson in early 1879. All 2000 inhabitants turned out for a roaring party which lasted several days. East of Tucson was the heart of Apache country. It was only a decade before when Chief Cochise had outrun and outgunned the U. S. Calvary in a series of vicious skirmishes.

Apaches or no Apaches, the Southern Pacific pushed on to the drowsing little border village of El Paso, reaching it in May, 1881, the end of the railroad's building charter. The next step had been long anticipated by Huntington, as he had already bought an interest in Thomas Peirce's road in Texas. The Southern Pacific crews continued building eastward from El Paso under the name of Galveston, Harrisburg and San Antonio while Peirce moved westward from San Antonio. The two railheads met on January 12, 1883. Los Angeles and California now had two transcontinental railroads; unfortunately both were controlled by the Big Four.

Huntington had effectively checkmated the Texas Pacific in every game they played. The smaller line never moved west out of Texas, and San Diego, the proposed Pacific terminal, was left without a railroad for a while longer. As happened to so many of the roads of the period, the Texas Pacific needed money badly in the eighties and mortgaged its subsidy lands. Subsequently, the railroad (no connection with the current Texas & Pacific) went bankrupt. The mortgaged lands were taken by the creditors and turned into the Texas Pacific Land Trust. As of 1971, stock certificate No. 390 of that trust remains unclaimed. Including principal and accumulated interest, it is worth $2,000,000 to the person who can prove he is the owner.

CHAPTER 17

"So many thousands of dollars on a useless mudhole like Wilmington Lagoon"

The Big Four had said in 1877 that grass would grow in the streets of Los Angeles. While it very nearly did for a variety of reasons, the Southern Pacific still went ahead with its plans for building a new railroad depot. With the commercial expansion of the town and inadequate space for switching of freight cars and rolling-stock maintenance, a new railroad depot, freight station and switching area was set up in 1878 north of College Street near what the old settlers still called San Fernando Street but which by 1876 was referred to as Upper Main Street (North Spring).

The old depot location at Alameda and Commercial streets was bought by Isaac Lankershim and Isaac Newton Van Nuys for $17,500. They built a flour mill on the site to process the wheat of the San Fernando Farm Homestead Association, of which they were two of the partners. Pio Pico had sold some 60,000 acres to the Association in 1869 for $115,000, a high sum for a semi-arid deserted valley covered with wild mustard and oats. This area in later years was to become Van Nuys, North Hollywood, Reseda, Canoga Park and Encino. Under the direction of Lankershim and Van Nuys, who had been much impressed with the height of the wild oats, the thousands of acres were plowed and seeded to wheat using phalanxes of eight-horse teams moving slowly across the flat valley floor. After Senator Charles Maclay and his partner, George K. Porter, bought the upper half of the San Fernando Valley (some 56,000 acres) from the heir of Eulogio de Celis for $80,000, they also planted the land to wheat. The San Fernando crop was a success, with production in the southern half of the valley reaching a half million bushels annually in a few years. Vessels left San Pedro for England and Europe loaded with both wheat and flour milled at the old station site at Commercial and Alameda in Los Angeles.

The new Southern Pacific depot location further solidified the commercial and shopping area along Main Street for a few blocks near the Plaza, in spite of the fact that for years many people had been predicting the center of town would move south. Calle de Los Negros and the streets west and north of the Plaza, particularly Bath Street (North Main), were, according to the Los Angeles *Star*, "notoriously infested with shameless bawds"[1] and a good many other characters much less attractive. But as occurred similarly some generations later, a number of people were determined to save the "central city" of the day. Pio Pico loved the area. He took the cash from the sale of his portion of Rancho San Fernando and announced the construction in 1869 of the first real hotel in town, on the corner of Main and Plaza streets on the site of the Carrillo town house. The Pico House was the first three-story building in Los Angeles, and the hotel was considered a solid sign of boom and progress when it was completed in 1870. Built of stuccoed brick around a center court, the entrance was on Main Street, opening into an impressive lobby with heavy rugs, leading up a double staircase to the second floor. The building was gas-lit, but the Los Angeles *Daily News* was more impressed with the fact that on the second and third floors there were "bathrooms and water closets for both sexes, convenient of access and approachable in strictest privacy."[2]

The Merced Theater was built next door to Pico's hotel on Main Street and opened New Year's Eve of 1870, with the Drum Barracks' band playing on the outside balcony before the first performance started. William Abbott built the theater and named it after his wife. Her only stipulation was that the building be a few feet higher than Pico House. The theater was moderately successful for a time, but neither Abbott nor his wife had any real flair as theatrical producers. By the mid-seventies it was called Wood's Opera House, featuring show skits changing weekly, with a flourishing bar which included some of the bawds from Bath Street. An added feature of the opera house was a cannon mounted outside the bar on a wooden platform. The cannon, which used blanks, was fired on what the proprietors or the chief bartender considered to be appropriate occasions.

With much local applause for his civic progressiveness and confidence in the future of Los Angeles, Colonel R. S. Baker further solidified the central area of the town around the Plaza area. He began the construction of the $110,000 Baker Block in 1877 on the site of Palacio de Don Abel at the corner of Main and Arcadia streets. The traffic lanes going east on the present San Bernardino Freeway cross the Baker Block location.

Arcadia Bandini de Stearns had married Baker three years before. At the time she was forty-seven, and he was forty-nine. Arcadia, still with the grace and poise of her youth, was "opulent and accomplished."[3] Baker had followed the Gold Rush to California and then had prospered with the wool boom. Arcadia, an unusual woman, continued to have things named after her. Baker, along with Senator John P. Jones, had been instrumental in laying out Santa Monica. In 1887 Baker built a very large and rambling resort hotel on the Palisades which naturally was called the Arcadia Hotel. He apparently was determined to duplicate or exceed anything that Abel Stearns had done for Arcadia until his death in 1894. Arcadia had no children from either the Stearns or the Baker marriage. She retained in her own name Rancho Laguna and other holdings from her marriage with Stearns, and Baker's estate was settled without problems after his death.

On September 15, 1912, Henry W. O'Melveny entered in his journal: "Arcadia Bandini de Baker died at 9:15 A.M. I was telephoned the sad news."[4] The South Coast knew that the last major personality of the Californio era was gone. The funeral was held at St. Vibiana's Cathedral with more than 2000 people in attendance, of whom eighty were relatives. Inconceivable as

it may sound, with the enormous value for the day of the
$7,000,000 estate, Arcadia died without a will. The probate and
litigation were guaranteed to engender bitterness among the
potential heirs and enrich the lawyers involved. Abel Stearns,
dead forty-one years, had forty-one blood descendants who were
eager to participate in the estate, with considerable legal justifica-
tion. Including the Bandini and Baker estate claimants, there
was a total of eighty-six potential heirs. After extensive litigation
and bargaining, the Bandini group received the lion's share. The
prime asset of the estate was Abel Stearns' gift to Arcadia of the
11,000-acre Rancho Laguna bounded by present-day Montebello
to the north, Bell to the south and Pico Rivera and Vernon approximately east and west respectively. This land was worth
perhaps eighty cents an acre in 1857, and the 8000 acres which
Arcadia still held was valued in 1912 at $5,600,000. In the 1960s
the going price for a good part of the old rancho was in the
order of $70,000 an acre.

Los Angeles was proud of its ornate new Baker Block and
considered it "the finest architectural ornament our city can
boast."[5] What would later be called an early Victorian mon-
strosity, the large three-story building had mullioned windows
behind pillars, the inevitable turrets topped with flagpoles and a
wind-finder on the main tower. Particularly impressive to a town
used to rough wood flooring was a huge entrance hall with a
marble floor and two marble stairways. The open-grillwork
elevator would come later. The Bakers had a large and luxurious
apartment on the third floor surrounded by a wide promenade
containing potted plants. The third floor also contained a number
of apartments for carefully selected tenants, and immediately the
Baker Block became the new social center for the South Coast.
New Year's Day in the seventies and eighties was the day to
have open houses in Los Angeles, and the residents joined hands
for a Baker Block party for the town society. It was an infinitely
quieter celebration and certainly not nearly as much fun as the
legendary fandangos which had occurred on the same site a generation or more earlier. The second floor of the Baker Block was
arranged for offices, with the prime space having elegant marble

mantles and grates along with washbowls, running water and gas. The lower floor was commercial space, with well-known names of the future like Germain, Rowan and Coulter opening up shops.

With all of this sedate civic progress, it was reasonable to presume that some limited attention would be given to the public school system, or lack of it, in Los Angeles. There had been talk since before the Civil War about having a public high school in Los Angeles. For a long time it was wishful thinking, as the Board of Education was having enough difficulty in appropriating money to pay the elementary school teachers, and three-fifths of the town's children attended no school at all. Finally in 1870, the state legislature appropriated $20,000 for a high school. The two-story frame structure with a cupola was built at Fort (Broadway) and Temple streets on Poundcake Hill, and the first real high-school classes opened three years later when Dr. W. T. Lucky, a professional teacher, was appointed superintendent of schools. The town felt it was truly making educational progress when the state legislature appropriated money in 1881 for a normal school (teachers college). The college's three-story brick structure, with the usual tower and peaked roof, was built on the site of the public library at Fifth and Charity (Grand) streets.

As for a library, there had been abortive attempts for years to have one. A subscription movement finally met with some success after the construction of the first high school, and library quarters were taken in four small and dark rooms in the Temple Block. Two years later, in 1874, a public library supported by tax moneys was established. About the same time Mrs. Caroline Severance, who had moved to Los Angeles from Boston, began energetically promoting the idea of a public kindergarten. In the mid-eighties this new idea was introduced as an experiment in the public schools.

During the cattle-boom days for the Californios, a Catholic school, St. Vincent's, had been opened in the old Lugo townhouse near the Plaza. After the end of the Civil War, the Bishop of Monterey and Los Angeles, Thaddeus Amat, pushed hard for public support of a college to be added to St. Vincent's. Two parcels of land were donated by O. W. Childs: the square block between Sixth and Seventh streets where Bullock's is today, and another block west, planted to oranges, where the Los Angeles Athletic Club building stands. By the end of the seventies, elementary, high-school and college classes were being held in a three-story brick building facing on Sixth Street.

Bishop Amat was an organizer and a fund raiser. He was determined to build a church in Los Angeles which he would call the Cathedral of Sancta Vibiana. The original site on Main Street between Fifth and Sixth streets was determined to be too far out of town. The cornerstone was laid at the present location near Second and Main streets in 1871. In the best tradition of major church building, the money that had been raised ran out when the time came to put a roof on the walls. But finally the building, similar in design to Barcelona's Puerto de San Miguel, was dedicated in 1876. About this time the Episcopalians bought a site for their procathedral on Olive Street across from the new Sixth Street or Central (Pershing Square) Park. The Common Council had agreed to fence and plant the square block of park when the land had been purchased by public subscription for $800 in 1870.

While there were mild signs of civic progressiveness, Los Angeles was still a scruffy little town of 5700 people in 1870, with only 15,000 people in the entire county, including Orange County of later years. A decade later the town's population was only 11,000 and the county's was 33,000. The town-hall location had followed a casual and peripatetic path from the original adobe room with a dirt floor across from the Bella Union Hotel in the fifties. By the early seventies, the location was at Spring and Jail (Franklin) streets in a one-story adobe below Poundcake Hill, with the city jail behind it in a separate building. As Boyle Workman described it: "The Council Room was dirty and dark, and made darker by a porch across the front. However, it was considered quite elegant because it had a floor, even though the floor was rough planks which were not nailed too closely together. There were no chairs. The only provision for citizens who had business to present to that august body was a splintery old bench that stood against the adobe wall."⁶

In later years the town hall moved to the second floor of the Temple Block, then on to Second Street between Fort (Broadway) and Spring streets, and finally in the late eighties it moved into its own quarters, a new and massive red-stone building between Second and Third streets on Fort.

Town elections, or all elections for that matter, were casual and often fraudulent. There was no voter registration. In a close election, a candidate who would pay over two dollars for a vote was considered a spendthrift, and the price dropped down for warm bodies which could be kept sober long enough to stagger into the voting booth. Obviously, if a man could collect twice or oftener for his vote from the different candidates, he had demonstrated the potential instinct of an entrepreneur. Since the Democrats and Republicans had different-colored tickets, and the fee was not paid until the proper ticket was dropped in the ballot box, getting paid twice for a vote required some advanced planning. As always there were candidates with lean pocketbooks and limited popularity. One such decided to keep a list of people who had promised to vote for him after he had aggressively buttonholed the potential voters. The magic number of votes to win was a thousand, and he had more than that number of promises. His total in the election was only a few votes. Asked for his reaction to the monumental landslide for his opponent, his grim reply was: "I have a list of one thousand of the damndest liars that live in Los Angeles County."⁷

Civil service was much further in the future than voter registration in Los Angeles. When John Bryam was elected to complete a term as mayor in the late eighties ". . . he delivered himself into the hands of his enemies by appointing all six of his sons to the police force."⁸ Even the extremely strong stomach of the town thought this was stretching nepotism a bit, considering the small size of the police force, and Bryam was defeated for re-election. The Common Council established a paid police department in 1869. The first chief of police, or city marshal as the post was initially called, was William C. Warren, who was killed in a gun battle with one of his deputies shortly thereafter. He was the grandfather of Eugene W. Biscauliz, a well-known sheriff of the county many years later. Warren received no salary; his income was from fees and reward money, and he had seven paid deputies who worked on a two-shift basis.

Lack of voter registration combined with the spoils system and boodling periodically roused the citizens to righteous wrath. In 1879 a long resolution was overwhelmingly passed at a large public meeting which concluded with the chilling statement:

". . . first by civil law, if possible; but in the event of the failure of civil proceedings, then we shall stand pledged as men and citizens to use that higher law of self-protection, and bring all such public plunderers to speedy and condign punishment."[9]

The threat in the group's resolution was by no means idle. A good many attending the meeting had taken part in the violent vigilante work of the town some years earlier.

The only reason that Los Angeles had not burned to the ground any number of times, as San Francisco had during the same period, was that its buildings were made of adobe. In theory, the town had had a volunteer fire department since the 1850s, but in reality it was a rather disorganized bucket brigade. With the number of wooden structures built during the first boomlet after the Civil War, it was obvious to the Common Council in 1871 that provision should be made for some kind of organized volunteer fire operation. As usual in such matters, no money was appropriated. Finally, a four-wheel man-powered fire engine was purchased, primarily through donations from the Calle de Los Negros gamblers, saloonkeepers and whorehouses, along with the silver miners using their facilities. Also fines from the weekend sprees of the Sonorans and Indians were grudgingly added to the kitty by the Common Council. The high-polished brass engine was lovingly housed near the town-hall location of the time at Spring and Jail (Franklin) streets. Nearby Buffum's saloon was the rallying point for the young bloods who were volunteers for Engine Company No. 1. Logically, competition was needed, and another fire engine was quickly subscribed. The headquarters of Engine Company No. 2 was conveniently located near a bar in the basement of the United States Hotel. When the fire whistle went off, considerable money changed hands on Calle de Los Negros and Commercial Street as to which brigade would arrive first at the fire. Tactical review and mutual criticism between the two companies after the fire was at a neutral saloon. When the nucleus of a paid fire department was organized in 1876, many people in Los Angeles did not consider it progress.

By the early eighties there were not that many drunkenness fines collected from Indians—fines which could be used to buy new fire engines, or anything else for that matter. The reason was simple. Most of the Indians were dead. The terrible week-end scenes of drunken revels, knifings and casual murder were gone. These, along with smallpox and pneumonia, had solved the town's Indian problem. By the time Standing Bear of the Poncas and Sarah of the Northern Paiutes were on lecture tours in New England and gaining the attention of wealthy author Helen Hunt Jackson, the bulk of the surviving Indians were in areas away from the towns, primarily on rancherias or small reservations.

Mrs. Jackson roughed out *Ramona* after long conversations with Don Antonio F. Coronel and his wife at their adobe town house in Los Angeles. At Dona Coronel's suggestion many of the *Ramona* scenes were laid at Rancho Camulos near Newhall on the Santa Clara River. Helen Hunt Jackson's book, when published in 1884, was immediately a best seller. How much it accomplished for the California Indians was another matter. An ironic twist of the book's popularity was that it did serve as another strong vehicle for publicizing the physical attractions of the South Coast.

The continued tub-thumping of railroad and regional publicity extolling the wonders of California started flushing some unlikely birds into the South Coast as early as the seventies. Noteworthy were Count Karol Bozenta Chlapowski and his wife,

Helena Modjeska, the reigning queen of the Polish stage while in her mid-thirties, and an unusual entourage which included Henryk Sienkiewicz, the author of *Quo Vadis.*

The Modjeska group, as it was called, boarded a German ship for America in 1876, with the ultimate destination being Anaheim. They arrived at San Pedro in November and took a stagecoach on the roads axle-deep in mud to the German colony. The Chlapowskis bought a typical clapboard Anaheim house while the Count looked enthusiastically for land in this less than a paradise which they had discovered. He paid $4000 for forty-five acres along Center Street, and soon learned that the straw laid on the street during the summer to keep down the dust bred fleas in astronomical quantities. Mme. Modjeska, as she was known professionally, made the decision to go back to the stage in America not only because of the fleas but also because the group needed money. Less than a year after arriving in Anaheim she opened at the California Theater in San Francisco after having laboriously memorized her lines in English. She was an instantaneous success and for years thereafter was on tour as one of the great performers of her era. Chlapowski loved his adopted South Coast, and Mme. Modjeska herself became interested when they bought 560 acres in the Santiago Canyon of the Santa Ana Mountains during the eighties. She superintended building a sprawling and very expensive house designed by Stanford White surrounded by extensive planting which she called the Forest of Arden. The Chlapowskis were only the first of many artistic groups or individuals that would flock to the magic land of the South Coast to find their own glories or disillusionments.

Los Angeles had little comprehension of, and only tepid interest in, the development of a harbor in the estuary back of San Pedro. The prevailing feeling in the early 1870s was: "The government must have a great deal of money to waste, if it could spend so many thousands of dollars on a useless mudhole like the Wilmington Lagoon."[10] A few men like Benjamin D. Wilson and Phineas Banning thought otherwise. As all the southern and central sections of the state were represented in one congressional district by Colonel S. O. Houghton of San Jose, he was the logical man for the harbor enthusiasts to approach for a feasibility survey by the Government. Houghton was able to have the study authorized, and a detailed survey was made in 1869 by Major R. S. Williamson of the Army Corps of Engineers. It is interesting that then, as now, the Army Engineers worked closely with the Congress on pork-barrel river and harbor projects in the congressional districts.

The success of the San Pedro harbor project depended on the feasibility of using the daily tides of five to seven feet to scour out a ship channel. To do this, Major Williamson had to determine whether it was possible to stop up the tidal "leaks" economically. With the huge tidal swamp in the reaches of the back estuary, he estimated that 250,000,000 cubic feet of water daily passed in and out over the flats which lay between Dead Man's Island and Rattlesnake (Terminal) Island on one side, and along the mainland toward Point Fermin on the other. To stop up much of the tidal leaks, in order to concentrate the flow of water for the necessary scouring action in the ship channel, Major Williamson's report envisaged a 6700-foot rock-and-timber wall running along part of Rattlesnake Island and connecting seaward to Dead Man's Island. It was a bold concept, and difficult for any layman to visualize as being successful when he saw a depth of water at the entrance bar of only eighteen inches at low tide.

Congressman Houghton and Benjamin D. Wilson (who was also doing the effective railroad lobbying for Los Angeles) appeared before the 1871 River and Harbor Committee of the House urging an eventual $425,000 appropriation for the San Pedro harbor project, with an initial allocation of $200,000. The committee gave a "do pass" recommendation, and it was approved by the Congress the same year.

Construction work was begun shortly thereafter under the direction of Colonel George H. Mendell, Army Corps of Engineers. The prognosis of Williamson, the surveyor, was correct. The channel-scouring action worked, and his forecast that the set of the wave pattern and currents would carry the sand east

of the harbor's mouth was accurate, as evidenced by a superb
beach which built up on Rattlesnake Island. Colonel Mendell
then proposed two additional improvements. He recommended
extending the east jetty 400 feet seaward from Dead Man's
Island in order to cut down the southeast swells at the harbor
bar during the winter storms. His second proposal was to build
a 3500-foot jetty on the west or mainland side, in order to dam
up even more of the tidal water moving in and out of the
estuary. By 1886, some $350,000 had been allocated by the Con-
gress to complete substantially all of Mendell's recommendations.
The end result of the basic tidal scouring action at San Pedro
was impressive, as reported by Captain James J. Meyler, the
supervising Army engineer, near the end of the project:

> The channel has deepened, widened and straightened. Where
> we had depths from six to ten feet in 1871, we now have from
> sixteen to twenty feet, and the depth of eighteen inches on the
> bar has increased to at least fourteen feet. There are at present
> lying alongside the wharves in the inner harbor two four-masted
> schooners and a barkentine, which had draughts, when crossing
> the inner bar, of seventeen feet eight inches, 18 feet six inches
> and 18 feet three inches respectively. Up to the present time
> about 133,000 tons of stone have been placed in the breakwaters,
> and there have been excavated only about 177,000 cubic yards
> of material, about 58,000 cubic yards of which was stone from
> a ledge of rock crossing the channel at the inner bar. From a
> rough calculation, however, I estimate that at least 2,000,000
> cubic yards of material have been removed from the channel,
> over nine-tenths of which has been done independently of
> dredging or blasting, the result of construction alone—the channel
> scouring itself under natural causes. The improvements have
> rendered it possible for the usual trading vessels of the coast
> to enter at this point a safe enclosed anchorage, free of all
> exposure to storms, and to deliver freight without the use of
> lighters. The total number of exports and imports has increased
> tenfold since 1871. . . .[11]

Rather to its surprise, the South Coast discovered it had a
substantial harbor. As further tangible evidence, there was a
wooden lighthouse built on Point Fermin in 1874. The lighthouse,
still standing, remained in use until World War II. Oil lamps

were used for the light until 1925, and after that time, electricity replaced the oil beacon.

San Pedro came to life in 1880 when the Southern Pacific decided to extend its tracks across Wilmington Lagoon to Timm's Landing inside the new breakwaters. The first through passenger train entered the booming village two years later past the long new wharves loaded with lumber from the Northwest.

Mr. Banning's "goose pond" had grown considerably in size as the years passed. But it was still a long way from a real deepwater port.

CHAPTER 18

"I thought you'd cut your queue off, John"

In most instances the rancho lands of the Californios were in new hands a few years after the great drought of 1862-64. But some of the old ways held on for a considerable time: "In months when work was slack during the 1870s, the Pico, Arellanes and Morgana families of the San Fernando Valley would entertain one another in a round-robin fashion, feasting for a day or night, going home for a rest, and ten days later showing up at the next casa for more of the same."[1] To the amazement of the children a few of the old Californios insisted on using the old-fashioned carretas. There were still dueñas for young girls, although the custom was dying out. Fiestas were held, but the fandangos, the great horse races and the superb reata work were gone.

The new Californio generation had difficulty remembering the leagues of rancho land and the cattle on a thousand hills. Many of the new generation worked on sheep ranches and turned to farming but showed little aptitude for the early industries of the South Coast such as railroading. A number turned to crime as did Tiburcio Vasquez. Through the 1870s and into the 1880s, Californio names were prominent on the "wanted" lists of peace officers.

Some of the young Californios like Ygnacio Sepulveda, son of Jose Andres, moved into the mainstream of the activities of the South Coast and the state. Ygnacio, born in 1842, was educated in eastern schools, and the Los Angeles *Star* reported in 1863 that he was "a young gentleman of liberal education and good, natural endowments, already versed in legal studies"[2] when he was admitted to the District Court bar. After being elected a state assemblyman, Sepulveda became a District, then a County, Court Judge. It was his resolution and outright courage as a twenty-nine-year-old judge which forced a series of criminal indictments in the wake of the lynchings and brutalities of the 1871 Chinese Massacre, in face of strong undercover pressure in Los Angeles to bury the shameful episode. After fourteen years on the bench, Ygnacio Sepulveda became United States chargé d'affaires to the Mexican government. His career was outstanding, but he was an exceptional Californio for his generation. Another of his contemporaries, Tiburcio Vasquez, chose crime as a career and became the last great bandido of the South Coast.

Tiburcio Vasquez knew he was an important man when the state legislature appropriated $15,000 expense money and posted a $3000 reward for his capture in January of 1874. Five months later the reward was increased to $8000 if Vasquez was captured alive or $6000 if he was brought in dead. The bandido had attained his statewide notoriety while surrounding himself with an aura of charisma during the previous several years.

Vasquez along with his lieutenant, Cleovaro Chavez, organized a gang in the San Joaquin and Gilroy areas after the bandit leader had finished serving a second prison term in 1870. The sacking of the village of Tres Pinos near Hollister, leaving three residents dead, was only one of a series of lightning and successful raids as the months went by. Posses throughout the area were out after the gang and got nowhere. It became increasingly clear that Vasquez had an effective network of informants on posse movements and that he was building a reputation as a sort of Robin Hood of his day with the Californios and the Sonorans. In no sense was there the unanimity of public support for hunting down the Vasquez gang as had existed seventeen years earlier in a similar situation with Juan Flores and Pancho Daniel.

The South Coast took only a general interest in the growing Vasquez legend until the gang robbed a stagecoach on the Cerro Gordo trail to Los Angeles. The prominent silver-mine owner Mortimer Belshaw happened to be aboard the stage and lost a silver watch, twenty dollars and some new boots while gaining some specific instructions from Vasquez to carry more money with him on future stagecoach rides. After the stage robbery, rumors began making the rounds in Los Angeles that Vasquez was going to base his operations for a time in southern California, and that a network of informants had already been established.

Confirmation of these Vasquez rumors was not long in coming. Alessandro Repetto, an Italian, had a small, prosperous sheep ranch near El Monte. On an April morning in 1874 Repetto found himself staring into the muzzles of five Henry rifles. The Vasquez gang wanted money—not what Repetto might have hidden in his house but what he had in the bank in Los Angeles. It was very evident that the bandits were well familiar with the rancher's affairs. Repetto was hauled out into his front yard, lashed to a tree, pistol-whipped a bit and then warned that the next step was to hang him from a limb of the same olive tree to which he was tied if he did not do what he was told. The rancher shakily wrote a check for $800 and sent his young nephew to collect the cash at the Temple and Workman Bank. When the boy presented the check, trembling with fear and excitement after the six-mile ride, the teller called over F. P. F. Temple, the bank president. After some brief questioning, the boy blurted out the story, and Temple sent for Sheriff William R. Rowland. Talking it over, Temple and the sheriff decided to send the boy back with the money while Rowland organized a dragnet. The sheriff dispatched a horseman to El Monte to raise a posse and sent a squad of men up the Los Angeles River to block one escape route. He then hurriedly assembled seven men and headed out Aliso Street for the Repetto ranch, following the boy with the money.

As the posse came up the trail to the Repetto ranch, the gang's lookout spotted the plume of dust from the galloping horses. Vasquez swept up the money the boy had just delivered, and the bandits ran for their horses, leaving Repetto and his nephew unharmed. As the chase continued, the outlaws on fresh horses pulled away from the following posse. Vasquez, who was justifiably noted for his coolness, now added to his reputation. As the posse doggedly held on, but out of rifle range, the gang came up to a wagon with four passengers and proceeded to rob them with apparent leisureliness. Still further up the trail, they overhauled a lone horseman and did the same thing again. The posse held on the track of the bandits until dusk, then lost it in the Verdugo Hills.

The next morning, as the posse rode dejectedly toward Los Angeles, Sheriff Rowland knew he was coming into a hornets' nest of criticism compounded by hysteria. The town rapidly had managed to convince itself that mass raids were on the way which could speedily amount to an insurrection. The Los Angeles *Express* solemnly instructed its readers: "Every storekeeper should have arms for his store, and every citizen who has a gun should keep it charged ready for instant service at any moment."[3] It was this atmosphere which spurred the governor to increase the reward for Vasquez's capture to $8000, or $6000 if the bandit was brought in dead.

The huge reward accomplished its purpose. The ring of secrecy which had protected Vasquez in the past was broken by an informer. Word was passed to Sheriff Rowland that Vasquez was holed up in the house of Greek George, a former camel driver, located below the mouth of Nichols Canyon in the present Hollywood area. The sheriff was also warned that his movements were being watched closely by Vasquez supporters. Taking the information seriously, Rowland secretly assembled an eight-man posse. The members reported one by one with their horses, shortly after midnight, at Jones' Corral on Spring Street near Seventh, prior to leaving for Nichols Canyon. While this was going on, the sheriff ostentatiously made his normal nightly rounds in the town.

The trap was sprung by the posse the following afternoon. Commandeering a wagon driven by two Sonorans, the posse members stretched out in the back, and then told the frightened men at gunpoint to drive to Greek George's house. As the wagon rattled up to the front door, the men jumped from the back and scattered around the house. Finally alerted, the unarmed Vasquez dived through a window and ran for his horse. A shotgun blast brought him to his knees for a moment, but then he struggled on at a staggering run. As Vasquez neared the tethered horse, another posse member wounded the bandit leader in the shoulder with a rifle shot. Vasquez then surrendered. There were no other gang members with him, and as the bandit leader himself said, he had been a damned fool to be there alone. Still cool and poised after his capture, Vasquez advised the posse members clustered around him in broken English: "You dress my wound and nurse me careful. You boys get $8000. If you let me die, you get only six. You get $2000 for being kind."[4] The posse was kind not only for the money but also because Tiburcio Vasquez, only five and a half feet tall with small hands and feet, was a man who instinctively commanded respect.

Vasquez was treated not only with respect when he was brought to Los Angeles but almost with a hysterical adulation by a good number of women of the town, as the South Coast relaxed delightfully from its exaggerated fear of guerrilla warfare. After a San Jose trial based on the Tres Pinos murders, Tiburcio Vasquez was hanged in March of 1875. Cleovaro Chavez, his lieutenant, continued the same type of raids for a time thereafter, but Chavez did not have the wit, ability and charisma of his leader. By November, Chavez was dead—killed for reward money.

As late as the 1902 issue, the 1162-page Sears, Roebuck catalogue devoted thirty-seven of those pages to guns and ammunition. In contrast, the 1970 Sears catalogue, with a total of 1593 pages, had only four on that subject. There was good reason for the weapon emphasis in the early years of the Sears mail-order business. Most of the men in the American West which began at the Missouri and Texas frontiers carried guns for many years after the Civil War. The South Coast was no exception. Revolvers in the 1902 Sears catalogue started in price at $1.60 for a 32-caliber hand gun and went up to $15.40 for a 45-caliber Colt. A Model 1873 Winchester repeating rifle cost $12.50. The price of a Remington derringer was $5, and a "neat little vest pocket revolver . . . with a 1⅝-inch barrel"[5] was $1.75. There was an obvious and solid basis for a common expression in the West of the time—"hot as a two-dollar pistol."

With the widespread use of guns, it was inevitable that after the Civil War, shooting brawls and tragedies would plague Los Angeles, where the elements of frontier violence died hard. When Solomon Lazard gave a ball and dinner at the Bella Union Hotel in 1866, it was natural that Robert Carlisle, as well as Andrew J. King, the county undersheriff at the time, be invited. There had been a history of bad blood between these two, particularly relating to the sheriff's handling of the murder four years before of John Rains, Carlisle's brother-in-law. The two men began brawling until the fight was broken up by the other guests, and King later asserted he received a stab flesh wound from Carlisle.

At noon the next day the steamer passengers were assembling at the Bella Union Hotel for the stagecoach ride to San Pedro, and Main Street in front of the hotel was jammed with the usual steamer-day crowd. Robert Carlisle was standing at the Bella Union bar, when he saw in the bar mirror Frank and Houston King, brothers of the undersheriff, stalk through the swinging doors drawing their revolvers. Carlisle spun around, whipping out his own gun. As the other people in the bar dived for the floor and through the verandah-type windows to the street, Carlisle was slammed back against the bar by the first bullets which hit him. He did not go down, and one of his shots killed Frank King.

Walking through the acrid powder smoke in a strange crab-like fashion, Carlisle forced Houston King into the street while King's bullets continued to thud into Carlisle's body. As Carlisle reached the street, he pitched forward, and King ran up and swung his revolver down on the wounded man's head. The blow broke the gun, but for a moment it seemed to revive the dying Carlisle. As King and the spectators watched in horrid fascination, the gravely wounded man raised himself to a sitting position against the hotel wall. Holding his gun with both hands as blood spilled down his face from the cut on his head and pooled at his feet from the body wounds, he shot Houston King in the chest and collapsed. King staggered back from the impact of the heavy slug, spun and fell. The battle was over.

Carlisle was carried into the hotel and stretched out on a billiard table, where he died shortly thereafter. Houston King, although seriously wounded, eventually recovered and was acquitted of the shooting. Carlisle was buried from the Bella Union the day after the gun fight, and Frank King's funeral was from his brother's home two days later. With all of the fusillade of bullets, only one bystander was wounded and one stage horse was killed.

Hand guns were used by the men carrying them for a variety of purposes other than killing and maiming each other. Boyle Workman always liked to tell a mostly apocryphal story of one specialized use:

> Once a visiting Englishman registered at the Pico House and made inquiries for Hancock M. Johnston, son of General Albert Sidney Johnston, to whom he had a letter of introduction.
>
> Johnston immediately exerted himself to demonstrate true California hospitality to the visiting Britisher. One evening, after dining well, if none too wisely, they went to the Britisher's room in Pico House to enjoy some profound conversation.
>
> Imagine the Englishman's astonishment when, in the midst of a sentence, the affable and courteous Johnston suddenly drew his pistol, shot at the Englishman's leg, and then calmly finished his sentence.
>
> Recovering his breath, the Engilshman indignantly asked Johnston what he meant by such a proceeding.
>
> "I'm not going to allow any damned cockroach to crawl up the leg of a man with a letter if introduction to me," answered Johnston.
>
> It seems that Johnston had noticed an offending cockroach on the British trousers and had neatly shot off the intruder without touching the clothing.[6]

Los Angeles hotel cockroaches were certainly noted for their size, but the insect Johnston presumably shot must have been very large indeed. Most travelers in the town were more impressed by the number and biting ability of the fleas.

Guns and violence had never been far below the surface in Los Angeles for many years. Joseph F. Dye, a policeman, represented both before Mason Bradfield killed him. Joe Dye and the first chief of police in Los Angeles, William C. Warren, fell into a heated argument over reward money in 1870. They shot it out at Temple and Spring streets, with Warren being killed and several bystanders wounded. Dye, a notoriously hot-tempered and trigger-happy man, was acquitted. Three years later, William R. Rowland, the new sheriff of the county at the time, tangled with Dye in front of the Orient Saloon, some yards from the previous shooting episode. Rowland threw a punch at Dye and found himself "seized by his handsome beard [and] covered by a cocked revolver."[7] The new sheriff fortunately did not reach for his gun, and stood Dye off. Mason Bradfield, nephew of the slain chief of police, began to annoy Dye after this episode to the extent that word was passed to the young man to stay out of the policeman's way or get himself killed.

Bradfield reached his own decision. He would ambush Dye. Finding out that the deputy commuted into town daily on the new railroad, he rented a room on the second floor of the White House Hotel at Commercial and Los Angeles streets. As Dye walked up Commercial toward the police station, Bradfield leaned out of the window of his room and killed Dye with a blast from a sawed-off shotgun. He stood trial for the murder and was acquitted.

Michael Lachenais was not as fortunate as Mason Bradfield. Lachenais attained the distinction of being the last person hanged by a vigilante committee in Los Angeles. When drunk and armed, he was a dangerous fellow and had previously been acquitted of the killing of a fellow Frenchman at a family wake. In 1870 he quarreled with his partner in a sheep-raising venture south of town. After moodily drinking in a number of the local saloons, he rode out to the sheep ranch and shot his partner to death. Sometime later Lachenais drunkenly babbled about the murder and was arrested. After word of the arrest was passed around town, a mass meeting was called at Stearns Hall, and a vigilante committee formed under the leadership of Felix Signoret. Several hundred armed men marched on the jail, hauled an alternately screaming and crying Lachenais two blocks to the Tomlinson & Griffith Corral on Temple above New High Street and hanged him from the crossbar over the gate. It was the last vigilante hanging, but the crossbar at the corral which had been utilized so often by mobs in the past was used again a few months later in a sorry and disgraceful episode involving the Chinese.

There were five to ten thousand Chinese, practically all men, in California after the start of the Civil War. These Chinese had first been recruited around the swarming ports of Canton and Hong Kong a decade earlier to do pick-and-shovel and coolie work in the gold fields. In the intervening time, many of them had scattered about the state in clusters, living and encouraged to live as complete aliens in a foreign land.

Charles Crocker made a decision for the Central Pacific Railroad in 1865 which eventually solidified the prejudice of most of the people in the state against the Chinese as a group. With labor unobtainable to build the railroad over the Sierras, Crocker began hiring pilot gangs of California Chinese. Tremendously pleased with their performance, he planned to use a maximum of 15,000 Chinese on the railroad and nearly reached that figure. Ships jammed with Cantonese men began to arrive in San Francisco from Hong Kong. By early 1869, Crocker's requirements for labor started to taper off, and the Chinese who had been working on the railroad began to settle around the state, taking any manual jobs where industry, patience and devotion would provide a living. Around this time serious mutterings of the "Yellow Peril" were heard.

For several generations after the Civil War, the Chinese in California were in a worse position than the newly freed slaves in the South. They were complete outlanders and were ineligible for citizenship. They were subject to registration as aliens and deportation on a casual whim, and with their long hair in the traditional queues, they were the readily available butt for torment by the inevitable petty bullies or drunks. Part of a song of the period called "John Chinaman" epitomized the crystallization of an underlying popular prejudice against them throughout the state:

> I thought you'd cut your queue off, John,
> and don a Yankee coat,
> And a collar high you'd raise, John,
> around your dusky throat.
>
> I imagined that the truth, John,
> you'd speak when under oath,
> But I find you'll lie and steal too—
> Yes, John, you're up to both.
>
> Oh, John, I've been deceived in you,
> and in all your thieving clan
> For our gold is all you're after, John,
> to get it as you can.[8]

As the Chinese fanned out over the state in their substantially increased numbers running laundries, other tiny shops and truck gardens as well as doing any kind of manual and field labor, the mutterings of hatred against them became a sullen chorus which could turn into a mob crescendo at any time. Living in a distant and hostile land with few of their own women, the Chinese became more withdrawn, more incomprehensible, and more susceptible to the vicious rumors of their enemies. Most Californians found themselves irrationally hating the Chinese as a group while loving many of them individually.

Probably the first Chinese to come to Los Angeles was a servant for Joseph Newmark in 1854. Newmark paid extremely well—$100 a month—which reflected the scarcity of competent household help in the small town along with the short-term cattle prosperity. By 1860 there was a beginning of a Chinese colony which settled in crumbling adobe warrens around Calle de Los Negros, with the first Chinese store being opened by Chun Chick the following year. Mah-jongg was the tremendously popular evening game of the Cantonese, and the sound of tiles being slammed on the tables was reminiscent of Hong Kong or Canton. As the years went by the Chinese settlement in and around Calle de Los Negros continued to grow, as the Chinese straggled into Los Angeles from working on the Southern Pacific.

The vigilantes were out in force in the early seventies, and Los Angeles again was in a "hanging mood" after the lynching of Michael Lachenais. Mob violence was just below the surface veneer of police control. Also tension was building up in the Chinese ghetto itself, centering on a few young Chinese women who had arrived from San Francisco. When one of the two chief tongs or companies—the Hong Chow—married a woman to a member, the Nin Yung tong began to buy revolvers. The tong war started with shots at the Hong Chow leader on October 23, 1871. The next day there was intermittent sniping and brawling between the two tongs. In the late afternoon a mounted policeman came charging into a swirling group, then dismounted and chased one of the Chinese into the dilapidated Coronel Building, which was at the head of Los Angeles Street and also fronted on Calle de Los Negros. The old main hall of the building echoed with several shots, and the wounded policeman staggered out of the doorway. A bystander came up to help the policeman and was killed. The Chinese then began wildly shooting at the crowd which had gathered in the street. Several were hit and the spectators scattered, but not for long.

Saloons emptied and shops were closed. In the early evening dusk a heavily armed crowd swirled around the Coronel Building and up Calle de Los Negros. The transformation to a blood-thirsty mob attacking the hated Chinese began when a door opened in the Coronel Building and a Chinese attempted to run out. He fell riddled with bullets. In the next few hours, despite the efforts of men like Sheriff James F. Burns, Robert and William Widney, Samuel B. Carswell and District Attorney Cameron E.

Thom, the mob of screaming, cursing men moved on its own frenzied and wild course of murder and pillaging. Frightened Chinese were hauled from their hiding places, ropes were thrown around their necks, and they were hanged from any improvised gallows at hand. Four were lynched on a large wagon, six from a wooden awning on Los Angeles Street and five at the Tomlinson & Griffth Corral. Looting accompanied the shooting and hanging as the beserk mob coursed through Chinatown.

The next day showed a body count of nineteen Chinese (initially reported higher than that), and headlines throughout the United States covered one of the worst mob episodes in the nation's history. No action was taken against the mob and its leaders, until a reluctant grand jury, yielding to Judge Ygnacio Sepulveda's unrelenting pressure, handed down nearly 150 indictments. Only nine were convicted, and they were released in a year's time. There was a massive lassitude and disinterest on the part of most of the Los Angeles community regarding the whole Chinese Massacre subject. One can readily suspect that a good many worthy citizens had as much or more responsibility for the massacre as the scum and underworld characters of Calle de Los Negros who were popularly blamed. The massacre represented, for the period, the high-water mark for violence and murders in Los Angeles.

The number of these crimes decreased sharply in the years immediately following the deadly episode, and even the notorious Calle de Los Negros simply became an extension of Los Angeles Street to the Plaza in 1877. However, for several more generations the Los Angeles Chinese continued to congregate in the general Plaza area. The Dakin Atlas of 1888 in its detailed map of this location showed a solidified Chinatown in the rectangle of Marchessault, Alameda, Aliso and North Los Angeles streets, with even special parcel wordings such as "opium joint" and "gambling." Also shown on the map in this area is a "Nigger Alley" from Plaza Street on the south side of the Plaza to Alameda Street. This was known as Ferguson Alley by the early twentieth century.

"He was driven to his death by the scoundrels who managed the bank"

William Workman committed suicide on May 17, 1876, at his Rancho Puente. The revolver shot was the official epitaph to the financial collapse of the South Coast's first boomlet. The suicide of the highly respected Workman, a contemporary of Abel Stearns, had its genesis over a score of years earlier when Francis P. F. Temple, the younger brother of John, married Antonia Margarita, Workman's daughter. F. P. F. Temple was a short man—five feet four—and called Templito by his host of Californio friends who found him modest and generous almost to a fault. After his marriage Temple lived on Rancho Merced, running cattle there as well as on several other ranchos.

With the end of the cattle period and the start of the business revival, Temple began to eye the developing commercial activities of Los Angeles. When Isaias W. Hellman in 1868 suggested a banking venture, he jumped at the idea. Riding out to Rancho Puente, Temple convinced Workman, his father-in-law, that he should become a partner in the proposed venture even though he (or for that matter, Temple) had no commercial, let alone bank, experience. The new bank was called Hellman, Temple and Company, and was organized shortly after John G. Downey opened the first bank in the town. The Hellman, Temple enterprise was located next door to the Bella Union Hotel, which by this time had grown to three stories and even had trees in front of it.

Hellman, a born banker, was less than impressed with F. P. F. Temple's business abilities as time went by, and the other partner,

William Workman, seldom stirred from Rancho Puente. Hellman finally told Temple two years after the start of the bank that a choice had to be made: Hellman would buy the Temple-Workman interests or Hellman would sell out to them. Reluctantly, Temple said he and Workman would sell. In 1871 John G. Downey and Isaias W. Hellman agreed to merge their two banks, and the resulting Farmers and Merchants Bank was located in the Downey Block. From the beginning, the two new partners made a smooth-working and successful team.

Meanwhile, in spite of Hellman's plain-spoken observations on his banking abilities, F. P. F. Temple still wanted a bank. Again he convinced his father-in-law to come into partnership with him, and he opened the Temple & Workman Bank in his fine new addition to the Temple Block in November, 1871. Henry S. Ledyard was hired as cashier and given the responsibility for day-to-day affairs. By Los Angeles standards, the bank's office appointments were elaborate and gave the impression of permanence and stability. Indicative of this was the counter built of well-fitted and finished cedar, a marked contrast to the usual bare or painted wood counters of the town. The bank did well. It certainly appeared that Temple's business ability had been misjudged, even though both Hellman and Downey still felt Templito was being far too liberal on his unsecured loans and that some of his investment-banking ventures were stretching far afield.

On the other hand, times were good, land prices were skyrocketing, and settlers were arriving in increased numbers on the South Coast. The Cerro Gordo water venture of Templito had been worrisome for a time, with investment input far higher than estimated. However, by May of 1874, water was being delivered in quantity to the Cerro Gordo mines. Temple readily admitted his deep involvement in the economic expansion of the South Coast. He remembered vividly the tight money and absurdly high interest rates of years earlier such as when his friend Jose Yorba had mortgaged 17,000 acres of Rancho Las Bolsas for $5500 at 5 per cent interest a *month*. Templito felt that the new settlers must be given the opportunity to buy land even if this meant taking a substantial amount of credit risk. When Temple rode out to the adobe at Rancho Puente, he had favorable news to report on the new bank's profitability to the aging Workman. Templito knew that people were saying he was an Abel Stearns of a new generation with a flair for seeing the South Coast's future.

The national panic of 1873 left a broad trail of financial wreckage and lost fortunes in most parts of the country. Yet California remained magically untouched and the business, mining and land boom seemed to spiral higher and higher. The people of California and eastern Nevada had convinced themselves that their economy would continue to move sharply forward on a broad front. The high priest of this philosophy was W. C. Ralston, president of the Bank of California in San Francisco. He was engaged in a pyramiding series of speculations in Nevada silver, and San Francisco business wildly expanded on an easy loan policy of his bank. Naturally, in its new-found commercial posture, little Los Angeles had to imitate San Francisco to a greater or lesser degree. F. P. F. Temple and his cashier, Ledyard, were in the forefront of the boom psychology.

California's speculative bubble burst in late August of 1875. Rumors had begun to spread in San Francisco about the solvency of the Bank of California; the result was a serious run on the bank, which was forced to suspend business. Shortly thereafter, W. C. Ralston's body was found floating off San Francisco's North Beach. A kind of "frenzy extended all over the state and every bank was obliged to close its doors."[1]

Shortly after news of the failure of the Bank of California clattered off the telegraph in Los Angeles, F. P. F. Temple and John G. Downey held a grim conference without Isaias W. Hellman, who was vacationing in Europe. The bankers could only hope the panic virus would not move south from San Francisco. It did. In the next day or so the riders on horseback or in spring wagons trooped into town to hear what was going on. The settlers clustered on the street corners and in the saloons talking about the gossip and rumors. They carefully read the

Farmers and Merchant Bank's special report: "Our bank was never in better condition; . . . we have now in our vaults as much coin as is needed for the transaction of our business."[2] The men also thought about the letters which had been drifting in from the East for two years on the effects of the business panic.

Lines began to form at the cashier windows of Los Angeles' two commercial banks to withdraw deposits. More important, men galloped out of town to report the lines were long and getting longer. As Downey and Temple watched the diminishing piles of gold pieces, word was passed to their friends to bring to the banks whatever cash they had. Initially, the money was sneaked into the back of each bank. Then the sacks of gold coins were carried in through the front doors in attempts to shore up depositors' confidence. Nothing worked to stop the withdrawals, as settlers swung off sweating horses to add to the lines in front of the banks' doors, but both banks made it through to the three-o'clock closing hour in the afternoon. Downey and Temple met that evening after the withdrawals of the day had been totaled up. Temple's situation was bad; Downey's condition was not good. A cable was sent to I. W. Hellman in Europe telling him that both banks would not reopen the next day.

The reaction of the town was initially fairly responsive to the announced moratorium. There was still the hope, as the Los Angeles *Star* put it, that " . . . trade will resume its customary channels and this passing ripple upon their surface will be forgotten."[3] Unfortunately, it was not a ripple; it was a full-scale tropical storm, as both Downey and Temple quickly learned. San Francisco, the commercial and financial center of the state, was in a state of shock and severe demoralization. "Save yourself, if you can"[4] was the watchword of the times. Cash was hoarded and loans were ruthlessly foreclosed. When Downey and Temple individually went north to San Francisco for funds, they got nowhere through ordinary channels. Finally, Downey received a $140,000 commitment from his brother-in-law, Peter Donahue, and Donahue's associates. This was forthcoming only because of family and strong political connections over the years. F. P. F. Temple was not so fortunate. Men who readily would have advanced hard cash on his and Workman's holdings two months before had no interest now.

While Downey and Temple frantically searched for money, I. W. Hellman began the long trip home to Los Angeles from Europe. He accomplished it in the remarkable time of twenty-three days, including stopping off at San Francisco, where he was able to get another cash commitment of $55,000. Hellman arrived by stage in Los Angeles on September 29 and was reasonably current as to the general financial situation in the state as a result of his brief stopover in San Francisco. Downey and he reviewed the Los Angeles situation in detail and the status of the bank's loans. It was clear now to both of them that if the Farmers and Merchants Bank was ever to reopen, now was the time. They agreed on a plan. Hellman would replace Downey as president. As a new arrival on the scene, Hellman would radiate confidence and help distribute the gold pieces from trays artfully arranged to give the appearance of more coin than there was. The plan worked when the doors of the bank swung open October 1. There was no run and deposits were well ahead of withdrawals.

On Spring Street the doors of the Temple and Workman Bank remained closed, while F. P. F. Temple continued his desperate search for money. He finally found Elias J. "Lucky" Baldwin, who was willing to make a loan. Baldwin had recently cashed out his controlling interest of the Ophir Mine in Nevada for over $5,000,000 and was well known for carrying large sums of cash with him in a tin money box. When he bought Rancho Santa Anita from H. Newmark & Company a few months before, the $12,000 down payment came out of the famous tin box. Baldwin was willing to advance Temple and William Workman $210,000, on two conditions: first, that they would give him a blanket mortgage on their combined real estate; and second, that their intimate friend, Juan Matias Sanchez, include in the mortgage 2200 acres of prime land near the San Gabriel Mission. Sanchez was deeply troubled about entering into the deal, telling Harris Newmark: "No quiero morir de hambre!"[5] But in the end Sanchez went along with mortgage plans for the sake of his old friends.

The doors of the Temple & Workman Bank were thrown open on December 6, with Templito greeting the customers, standing by the counters and their stacks of gold pieces which were taller than he was. There was no run on the bank and even some increase in deposits. That evening Temple's many friends sponsored a fine supper at the Pico House in honor of him and the reopening of the bank. At one o'clock the next morning the party broke up after three cheers for Temple and Lucky Baldwin. With both banks now open it seemed reasonable to expect the South Coast could get back to normal.

This was not the way it worked out. A quiet erosion of withdrawals began at the Temple & Workman Bank shortly after the celebration supper, and the withdrawal rate increased as the weeks went by. There was no proximate reason. Templito's popularity was at a new high. It was more of an individual depositor's decision that his money would be better cached at home or placed in the Farmers and Merchants Bank. There was an enveloping tide, and the cash Lucky Baldwin had advanced began to melt away like a child's sand castle. Another $100,000 advance from Baldwin accomplished nothing, and the Temple & Workman Bank closed its doors finally on January 13, 1876.

The receivers of the defunct bank found its affairs in a chaotic state. Temple, his cashier, Henry S. Ledyard, and even William Workman found themselves under a drumfire of criticism and abuse as the bank audit progressed, and with the passage of time, it was evident that little would be recovered from the bank assets. Lucky Baldwin foreclosed on his blanket mortgage, and Temple, Workman and Sanchez were landless and virtually penniless. While Workman had said little during the period of travail, unquestionably the most brutal blow of all was to see an old and cherished friend, Juan Matias Sanchez, lose his hereditary holdings. After Workman's suicide, the depth of feeling of some was indicated by the *Republican*: "He was driven to his death by the scoundrels who managed the bank, and they are responsible before God for his blood."[6]

F. P. F. Temple was a broken man. Shortly after William Workman's suicide he had a stroke. From that time Temple lived as a recluse with friends, and he died in 1880 in a sheepherder's hut in a corner of Rancho Merced. Temple Block, at Spring and Main streets and built by him and his older brother John, was included in the blanket mortgage given to Lucky Baldwin. This was sold at a sheriff's sale in 1877 to H. Newmark & Company.

The only thing which seemed to go right for the South Coast for a few years after the Temple & Workman Bank failure was the arrival of the Southern Pacific, and it was not long before local shippers bitterly discovered they were dealing with a powerful transportation monopoly.

One problem after another plagued the Cerro Gordo mines starting in late 1875, and rumors began to circulate that the principal ore body was nearing exhaustion. A year later the Union Mine closed down permanently just as a drought was developing on the South Coast.

The frightful stories of the lack of rainfall in the early sixties were told again and again. Men looked for the wind to haul around to the southeast, which was the real indication of a winter rainstorm. The sheepmen held on from week to week, waiting for the rains which did not come until December of 1877. Most of the sheep died. The valleys and hills were brown, and the ground crops began to wither. The new citrus groves were laboriously watered from barrels hauled from the shrinking rivers. Again there was smallpox, as in the long drought of the early sixties. However, with vaccines and existing immunities, the epidemic was not nearly as severe as the one of the previous decade.

With all of California feeling the delayed impact of the national panic of 1873, credit in Los Angeles and the South Coast was scarce and interest rates were high. The deadening effect on economic growth of railroad rates set at the maximum the traffic would bear was beginning to be felt. The boomlet was over, and the new railroad, for those who dreaded seasickness, served as a convenient and quick route to leave the South Coast. Los Angeles, which had a population of about 16,000 in 1876, found it had dropped to 11,183 four years later. Even the most optimistic land boomer could not ignore the For Sale and For Rent signs all over town. And by that time, in the sprawling acres of grapevines around Anaheim and several of the new towns nearby, there was worried talk of a blight which was attacking the oldest and strongest wine vines.

Yet with all the discouragements, the basis of a new South Coast had been well laid. Cheap and good land, the Washington navel orange, the fantastic vegetable crops in the old delta of present-day Orange County, the continuing publicity of endless sunshine and superb climate, and a railroad connecting the South Coast with the rest of a powerful and growing United States were the necessary building blocks.

Two more things were needed to bring the first real magic of the South Coast into being: a transcontinental railroad via the southern route and, much more important, aggressive competition to the Big Four. Collis P. Huntington and the Southern Pacific were well on their way to accomplishing the former, but they had every determination that the latter would not occur.

CHAPTER 20

"The train fare was first six dollars and, for a few hours, one dollar per head"

Perhaps the railroads believed some of their own propaganda as to the wonders and opportunities of the western half of the United States. Immediately after the Civil War a number of companies initiated promotions to build to the West Coast. Typical was the Atchison, Topeka and Santa Fe, chartered in Kansas in 1859. Nearly a decade later it finally began construction work toward Santa Fe, New Mexico; crossed Raton Pass in the Rocky Mountains; entered Santa Fe in 1880; and then tied into the Southern Pacific tracks at Deming, New Mexico. Using the old Atlantic and Pacific rights to build along the thirty-fifth parallel which had been picked up by the St. Louis and San Francisco group, the Santa Fe moved westward out of Santa Fe, obviously pointing toward the desert crossroads of Needles, California. Collis P. Huntington reacted to this threat to the Big Four's California monopoly, and a dead-end branch line was hurriedly laid across the desert from Mojave, the railhead of the Tehachapi spur, to Needles, on the west bank of the Colorado River. When the Santa Fe reached the east bank in 1883, there were two railheads staring at each other in the middle of nowhere with neither of them going anywhere.

The Santa Fe had no alternative but to fight the Southern Pacific to the bitter end for a Pacific Coast outlet. A retreat might very well be the finish of the road, with the competitor buying the company on a piecemeal basis for the cost of the rails. For some time the Santa Fe had been building northward toward the U. S. border from Guaymas, aided by Mexican

government subsidies with a planned tie-in to the Southern
Pacific at Benson, Arizona. But the Big Four had effective control because it could cancel the Santa Fe's rights from Benson
to Deming, New Mexico, at any time. The only remaining way
to attack the Southern Pacific was to move out from the sole
deep-water harbor south of San Francisco-San Diego Bay. This
would mean bringing equipment and material all the way around
the Horn, even though the Santa Fe's own railhead was moving
toward Needles, 385 miles away through Cajon Pass.

After the Gold Rush, it seemed inevitable to a number of
people, beginning with William H. Davis and later Alonzo E.
Horton, that San Diego would be the great gateway to the
Southwest. The serious development of San Pedro as a port
seemed patently absurd, and it seemed equally evident that
Los Angeles should continue to be an inland town with its
deep-water commerce funneling through San Diego. The news
of the effective lobbying work of Benjamin D. Wilson in 1871
for the Federal development of the San Pedro estuary as an
inner harbor was received in San Diego with almost disbelief.
It was finally evident to men like Horton that the town of 3000
population must have a transcontinental railroad to exploit its
magnificent harbor. There had been talk on several occasions
prior to the Texas Pacific of a railroad from the southwest to
San Diego, but nothing ever came of it. Even though the railhead of the Texas Pacific was 1300 miles away, when grading
for a roadbed started in town in 1873, it almost seemed as if
trains would be arriving any day from the East. However,
Collis P. Huntington killed this dream when the Southern Pacific
threw a bridge across the Colorado at Fort Yuma in 1877.

San Diego with its superb harbor was fresh out of railroads
in 1880 when the Santa Fe proposed the establishment of the
California Southern Railroad Company. A local subsidy, con-
tingent upon railroad performance, was agreed upon: $25,410
in cash, 17,355 acres of land, including some waterfront of the
Rancho de la Nacional (later named National City), and 485
city lots. The Santa Fe's initial and publicized plan for its
California Southern was simple: build a railroad from San Diego

to San Bernardino, which meant crossing the Southern Pacific rails at the new village of Colton. The proposed route would be north along the coast up to what is now Oceanside, then turning inland across the coastal mountains and up Temecula Canyon and then to Riverside before reaching Colton. The real objective was the Cajon Pass above San Bernardino, the upper desert and the planned Santa Fe railhead at Needles. The Santa Fe assigned one of their bright young men to build the 135-mile California Southern to San Bernardino, thirty-two-year-old Joseph O. Osgood. By March of 1881, Osgood had his construction gangs at work and rails were arriving from Europe along with the first locomotive shipped from the East Coast. By January of 1882, Osgood was laying tracks in Temecula Canyon and not following local advice to route the tracks considerably higher up the canyon side because of danger of winter floods. The line reached Colton on August 21, where it seemed for a time that the road would be stopped indefinitely.

Collis P. Huntington and Leland Stanford were not overly concerned with the California Southern gambit of the Santa Fe. They would never give permission for the Santa Fe tracks to cross the Southern Pacific at Colton. They felt that the opposition's inevitable appeal to the state courts could be readily handled. And finally, the Southern Pacific had a bagful of operating tricks to plague an overextended Santa Fe ranging from rate-cutting to buying control of the San Diego Steamship Company. The Big Four were right for nearly a year. Then the people of San Bernardino took matters into their own hands.

San Bernardino had been deliberately bypassed by the Southern Pacific as punishment for the town's aggressive support of John P. Jones in his fight against the Big Four. The new railroad townsite of Colton four miles south was supposed to dry up San Bernardino. The Santa Fe had been careful to let the people of San Bernardino know that a special crossing frog to go on the Southern Pacific tracks was sitting on a flatcar at the stalled railhead at Colton. It was also common knowledge in the town that reinforced train crews were riding spare Southern Pacific locomotives up and down the section of track to prevent the Santa Fe gangs from using the crossing frog. On a steaming August day in 1883 there was a mass meeting at the San Bernardino courthouse. Attendance ranged from newcomers to Rangers whose posses had chased outlaws over southern California and men who had fought running skirmishes with raiding Utes coming down the Cajon. There was shouted agreement at the meeting that the deadlock at Colton must be broken, by force if necessary. The Santa Fe rail gangs were alerted, and a large armed posse rode to Colton. The patrolling Southern Pacific locomotives were stopped with roadblocks and the rail crews warned off with rifles. The crossing frog was manhandled off the flatcar, and probably a record was set in installing it. While the posse patrolled the crossing, other citizens were airing their opinions forcibly with the local court. Two days later an injunction was issued against the Southern Pacific. By September 4, track was laid all the way from San Diego to a boxcar depot in San Bernardino.

The Santa Fe could now begin thinking about Cajon Pass and the high desert—at least until February of 1884, when the entire line through the Temecula Canyon was washed out exactly as Osgood, the engineer, had been warned might occur. The Santa Fe treasury was at one of its periodic low ebbs, and as a result it was nine months before San Diego had any rail service. Finally, the line was rerouted up through San Juan Capistrano, Santa Ana and Corona to Riverside.

The Santa Fe for a time considered utilizing the tunnel work on the west side of Cajon Pass which had stopped when Jones' Los Angeles and Independence Railroad had been bought up by the Southern Pacific seven years before. Finally, the engineering decision was made to make a deep cut on the east side of the pass to break through the rim of the high desert, and this is the route followed today.

By early November of 1885 the Santa Fe was through Cajon Pass and had reached the desert crossroads of Barstow. Needles and the idle railhead from the east was only 170 miles away. The Santa Fe, San Diego and San Bernardino had won. Bargaining to the last, a deal was finally made with the Southern

Pacific. On a reciprocal lease basis the Santa Fe turned over its Mexican interests, and the Southern Pacific gave up its Mojave-Needles tracks. The first through train for the East, consisting of a passenger coach and a mail and express car, left San Diego from the D Street depot on the evening of November 16, 1885. San Bernardino was ready with a band, a barbecue, fireworks and appropriate speeches when the train arrived there.

The saga of the Santa Fe and its struggles with the Big Four drew strong support throughout southern California. But over and above this, a substantial item of interest was the persistent rumor that some of the best food being served in the United States anywhere was on the Santa Fe. These rumors seemed too incredible to be even partially true. Food in the West was generally indifferent, and railroad food was notoriously bad. The privately owned eating houses on the railroad lines were dirty and " . . . often their owners were in cahoots with train crews. The charge was four bits (fifty cents) in advance. No sooner had the customer paid and started to eat, than the bell rang, the whistle blew and the passenger had to dash back aboard his train, most of his meal uneaten. The beanery then paid off the train crew at a dime a passenger and waited for the next victims."[1]

The rumors of good food with accompanying good service were true. An Englishman by the name of Fred Harvey began writing a chapter of the American West in 1875 when he opened the first Harvey House in the Topeka, Kansas, railroad depot. The Santa Fe's contribution was space and an assortment of materials and supplies. The depot restaurant was a resounding success, not only for the railroad passengers but also for the people of the little town of Topeka, who could finally get some decent food. As a result of this first success, Fred Harvey eventually took over all of the Santa Fe's restaurants and dining cars, where even the coffee was required to meet rigid and uniform standards. Both he and the railroad agreed that the dining-car service should not operate at a profit and that this ground rule would apply to certain of the Harvey Houses as well. Their rationale was that this decision would mean increased passenger travel and more freight business, and they were right. The menu for a seventy-five-cent dinner aboard a through Santa Fe train in 1888 was impressive, to say the least:

BLUE POINTS ON SHELL

ENGLISH PEAS AU GRATIN

FILETS OF WHITEFISH, MADEIRA SAUCE

POTATOES FRANCAISE

YOUNG CAPON, HOLLANDAISE SAUCE

ROAST SIRLOIN OF BEEF AU JUS   PORK WITH APPLESAUCE

TURKEY STUFFED   CRANBERRY SAUCE

MASHED POTATOES   BOILED SWEET POTATOES   ELGIN SUGAR CORN

MARROWFAT PEAS   ASPARAGUS, CREAM SAUCE

SALMI OF DUCK   QUEEN OLIVES

BAKED VEAL PIE ENGLISH STYLE

CHARLOTTE OF PEACHES, COGNAC SAUCE

PRAIRIE CHICKEN, CURRANT JELLY

SUGAR CURED HAM   PICKLED LAMB'S TONGUE

LOBSTER SALAD AU MAYONNAISE

BEETS

CELERY   FRENCH SLAW

APPLE PIE   COLD CUSTARD A LA CHANTILLY   MINCE PIE

ASSORTED CAKES   BANANAS   NEW YORK ICE CREAM

ORANGES   CATAWBA WINE JELLY   GRAPES

EDAM AND ROQUEFORT CHEESE

BENT'S WATER CRACKERS   FRENCH COFFEE

Wednesday, Nov. 14, 1888   *Meals 75 cents*

However, the Harvey Houses were more famous in western America than the dining cars. This was so because residents of an isolated area as well as the train passengers could get excellent meals served by the Harvey Girls. The restaurants were arranged along the railroad so that while the passengers ate, the locomotive and rolling stock could be watered, fueled and checked. Harvey dining-room meals in the seventies and eighties were fifty cents with standard entrees, and less at the lunch counter. At Holbrook, Arizona, just after the railhead had reached Needles on the California border, the dining room was in five battered boxcars. Inside there were the usual English silver, crystal, Irish linen and bouquets of fresh flowers. A mile from the Holbrook depot the engineer on an arriving train blew his whistle. This was the signal for the waitresses to place the first course on the tables while thick steaks of prime beef from Chicago were put on to fry.

The famous Harvey Girls, the waitresses of the Harvey Houses, were a trademark of the Santa Fe. About 5000 of them married men they met at the dining rooms and lunch counters in the small villages and towns along the railroad. The Santa Fe recruited the girls by newspaper advertisements in the Middle West and East, stating the basic requirements of "good character, attractive and intelligent, 18 to 30."[2] The girls lived in a rigidly supervised dormitory near the train restaurant, and except for special occasions, were required to be in the dormitory by ten o'clock at night. Starting wages were $17.50 a month plus tips and plus board and room, and the sought-after jobs were considered well paid for the day. The Santa Fe's problem was that their new recruits were continually quitting to get married. However, this in turn was one of the main reasons why recruiting was never much of a problem as word of the record number of marriages of the Harvey Girls in the storybook American West spread quickly to other parts of the country.

After completion of the through route from the East to San Diego, passengers and freight destined for the South Coast came off the Santa Fe at Colton and were handed over to an unfriendly Southern Pacific. As the Santa Fe had every intention of coming into Los Angeles, it decided to follow the plan of consolidating a number of short roads which had sprung up, such as the Los Angeles & San Gabriel. After a good bit of tidying up of these small lines, the Santa Fe arrived in Los Angeles via Pasadena on May 31, 1887, to the usual accompaniment of bands, speeches and beer. Another loop line by way of Riverside and Orange (tying into San Diego) and through to Redondo Beach was opened on August 12, 1888.

Even before it arrived in Los Angeles, the Santa Fe became involved in what appeared to be a disastrous and futile rate war for both passengers and freight with the Southern Pacific. In spite of all of the publicity and ecstatic letters home from settlers after the first rugged years, the population of Los Angeles County (which still included Orange County) in 1880 was only 33,000. The South Coast appeared to fall into the category of a misty distant Avalon of legend for the bulk of the people of the United States and Western Europe. Even the most stouthearted land boomer could see no more than a gradual growth for southern California. In the face of all of this, the two railroads began a deadly rate war.

The first-class fare between Chicago and San Francisco when the Pacific railroad opened in 1869 was $130. Four years later it was $118 and second-class was $85, and the fares held there until 1886. The Southern Pacific cut rates first, and the Santa Fe forthwith met the cut and went a good deal further. Near the end of 1886 the highest rate for a railroad ticket between the Pacific Coast and Missouri River points was fifteen dollars. Then the Santa Fe reduced it to ten dollars and on March 6, 1887, the train fare was first six dollars and, for a few hours, one dollar per head. Shortly thereafter the fare went up to twenty-five dollars, where it remained for nearly a year, and then to fifty dollars first class and forty dollars second class.

The fare battle between the two great railroads became national news. Suddenly, a long smoldering public interest generated by years of promotion of the South Coast became a crown fire. In tens of thousands of family homes in the Midwest and East, the decision was reached to buy the bargain railroad tickets and make a trip or move to southern California.

The railroads, to their own amazement, found they were adding section after section of sixteen-car "emigrant trains" pulled by two engines. Each car had folding seats which could be flattened into beds and a stove at the end of the corridor for cooking. It was highly social community living, in some ways similar to the wagon trains of years earlier.

Both the Santa Fe and the Southern Pacific also had hundreds of "Zulu" cars which operated in freight trains. One member of a family would ride in a Zulu car along with the family possessions and livestock while the rest of the family would be on an emigrant train.

Los Angeles was dazed by the influx of people. The Santa Fe had three or four trains a day arriving at its depot near the Los Angeles River. The Southern Pacific deposited 120,000 people in the town within a year's time.

As the tide of newcomers poured out of the emigrant trains and Zulu cars, Arcadia Bandini de Baker was celebrating her sixtieth birthday. She must have thought of the contrast between 1887 and forty-six years earlier when she married Don Abel Stearns at the church across from the Los Angeles Plaza in the remote Mexican province of Alta California. In the intervening years since her wedding California and the South Coast had had the excitement and good times through most of the 1850s, and the terrible times through the years of the 1860s. The boomlet of the 1870s had faded, and some of the old and familiar American names were gone—Stearns, Workman, Temple and even Phineas Banning, who, after several years of illness, died at age fifty-four and was buried in the new Rosedale Cemetery.

The newcomers of 1887 surging up and down the streets of the town, along with the rumble and clatter of arriving trains bringing still more people, gave ample evidence that Los Angeles and the South Coast were being precipitated into another beginning.

Source Notes on Quotations

CHAPTER 1

1. Cleland, *Cattle on a Thousand Hills*, 249-50.
2. Bell, *Reminiscences of a Ranger*, 198.

CHAPTER 2

1. Bell *Reminiscences*, 129.
2. Cleland, *Cattle*, 140-41.
3. Ibid., 93.
4. Los Angeles *Star*, May 10, 1856.
5. Cleland, *Cattle*, 92-93.
6. Los Angeles *Star*, Jan. 31, 1857.
7. Ibid.

CHAPTER 3

1. Bell, *Reminiscences*, 301.
2. Cleland, *Cattle*, 74.
3. Los Angeles *News*, Feb. 11, 1869.
4. Cleland, *Cattle*, 82.
5. Los Angeles *News*, Feb. 11, 1869.
6. Bell, *Reminiscences*, 36.
7. *Out West*, Apr. 1909, 307-8.
8. Sanchez, *Spanish Arcadia*, 370.
9. Newmark, *Sixty Years in Southern California*, 160.
10. Cleland, *Cattle*, 145.
11. Los Angeles *Star*, Apr. 26, 1856.

CHAPTER 4

1. Pitt, *Decline of the Californios*, 84.
2. Cleland, *Cattle*, 49-50
3. Meadows, *Orange County*, 89.

4. *Southern Californian,* Apr. 11, 1855.
5. Gillingham, *Rancho San Pedro,* 112.
6. Ibid, 156.
7. Ibid., 175.
8. Pitt, *Decline of the Californios,* 89.
9. Cleland, *Cattle,* 86.

CHAPTER 5

1. Bell, *Reminiscences,* 2-6.
2. Cleland, *Cattle,* 205.
3. Newmark, *Sixty Years,* 307.
4. Cleland, *Cattle,* 167.
5. Dana, *Two Years Before the Mast,* 277.
6. Davidson, *Directory for the Pacific Coast,* Appendix 44.
7. Willard, *Free Harbor Contest,* 27.
8. Bell, *Reminiscences,* 336.
9. Ibid.

CHAPTER 6

1. Bell, *Reminiscences,* 5-7.
2. Guinn, *Historical and Biographical Record,* 108.
3. Bell, *Reminiscences,* 35.
4. Los Angeles *Star,* Nov. 19, 1862.
5. Newmark, *Sixty Years,* 141
6. Bell, *Reminiscences,* 175.

CHAPTER 7

1. Cleland, *Cattle,* 107.
2. Ibid., 108.
3. Ibid., 107
4. Newmark, *Sixty Years,* 165.
5. Ibid., 204.
6. Ibid.
7. Los Angeles *Star,* Jan. 4, 1855.

CHAPTER 8

1. Newmark, *Sixty Years,* 337
2. Ibid.

CHAPTER 9

1. Los Angeles *Star*, Apr. 22, 1856.
2. Cleland, *Cattle*, 88-89.
3. Los Angeles *Star*, Apr. 22, 1856.
4. Cleland, *Cattle*, 148.
5. Los Angeles *Star*, Jan. 25, 1862.
6. Cleland, *Cattle*, 174.
7. *Southern News*, Jan. 22, 1864.
8. Cleland, *Cattle*, 262-64.
9. Gillingham, *Rancho San Pedro*, 253.
10. Cleland, *Cattle*, 183.

CHAPTER 10

1. Oscar Lewis, *Big Four*, 321.
2. Wilson, *Southern Pacific*, 1.
3. Lewis, *Big Four*, 35.
4. Ibid., 64.
5. Ibid., 347.
6. Wilson, *Southern Pacific*, 59.

CHAPTER 11

1. Cleland, *Irvine Ranch of Orange County*, 140.
2. Bixby-Smith, *Adobe Days*, 32.
3. Ibid., 29.
4. Ibid., 36-37.
5. Ibid., 84-85.
6. Ibid., 65.
7. Ibid., 60.
8. Newmark, *Sixty Years*, 439.
9. Ibid., 437-38.

CHAPTER 12

1. Cleland, *Cattle*, 269.
2. Ibid., 270.
3. Nadeau, *City-Makers*, 20.

CHAPTER 13

1. Hornbeck, *Roubidoux's Ranch,* 151.
2. Ibid., 117.
3. Ibid., 164.
4. Cleland, *Cattle,* 232.

CHAPTER 14

1. Nadeau, *City-Makers,* 32.
2. Ibid., 64.

CHAPTER 15

1. Los Angeles *Star,* July 28, 1860.
2. Nadeau, *City-Makers,* 28.
3. Newmark, *Sixty Years,* 469.
4. Tompkins, *Little Giant of Signal Hill,* 73.

CHAPTER 16

1. Nadeau, *City-Makers,* 58.
2. Wilson, *Southern Pacific,* 61.
3. Nadeau, *City-Makers,* 143.
4. Ibid., 144.
5. Newmark, *Sixty Years,* 504.
6. Ibid., 506.
7. Ibid., 507.
8. Nadeau, *City-Makers,* 151.
9. Newmark, *Sixty Years,* 505-6.

CHAPTER 17

1. Robinson, *Los Angeles from the Days of the Pueblo,* 69.
2. Los Angeles *Daily News,* May 25, 1870.
3. *Illustrated History of Los Angeles County,* 702.
4. Clary, *History of the Law Firm of O'Melveny,* 205.
5. Los Angeles *Evening Express,* Aug. 6, 1877.
6. Workman, *City that Grew,* 106.
7. Ibid., 174.
8. Ibid., 238.

9. Los Angeles *Evening Express*, Feb. 1, 1879.
10. Willard, *Free Harbor Contest*, 36.
11. Ibid., 39.

CHAPTER 18

1. Pitt, *Decline of Californios*, 252.
2. Newmark, *Sixty Years*, 315.
3. Nadeau, *City-Makers*, 98.
4. Ibid., 99.
5. *1902 Sears, Roebuck Catalogue*, 318.
6. Workman, *City that Grew*, 41.
7. Nadeau, *City Makers*, 95.
8. McWilliams, *Southern California Country*, 92.

CHAPTER 19

1. Newmark, *Sixty Years*, 478.
2. Nadeau, *City-Makers*, 133.
3. Ibid., 134.
4. Newmark, *Sixty Years*, 478.
5. Ibid., 479.
6. Nadeau, *City-Makers*, 139.

CHAPTER 20

1. Marshall, *Santa Fe*, 98.
2. Ibid., 100.

Bibliography

Bancroft, Hubert Howe, *California Pastoral*. San Francisco, History Co., 1888.

Bandini, Helen Elliot, *History of California*. New York, American Book Co., 1908.

Bascom, Willard, *Waves and Beaches: The Dynamics of the Ocean Surface*. Garden City, N.Y., Doubleday, 1964.

Bell, Horace, *On the Old West Coast*. New York, Grosset & Dunlap, 1930.

————, *Reminiscences of a Ranger*, orig. ed., 1881. Santa Barbara, Calif., Walter Hebberd, 1927.

Bigger, Richard, and Kitchen, James D., *How the Cities Grew*. Los Angeles, Univ. of California, 1952.

Bixby-Smith, Sarah, *Adobe Days*. Cedar Rapids, Iowa, Torch Press, 1926.

Carrillo, Leo, *The California I Love*. Englewood Cliffs, N.J., Prentice-Hall, 1961.

Chalfant, W. A. *The Story of the Inyo*. Chicago, Hammond Press, Chicago, 1922.

Clary, William W., *History of the Law Firm of O'Melveny & Meyers*. Pasadena, Calif., Castle Press, 1966.

Cleland, Robert Glass, *The Cattle on a Thousand Hills*. San Marino, Calif., Huntington Library, 1941.

————, *The Irvine Ranch of Orange County*. San Marino, Calif., Huntington Library, 1952.

Combs, Barry B., *Westward to Promontory*. Palo Alto, Calif., 1969.

Dana, R. H., *Two Years Before the Mast*. New York, Grosset & Dunlap, 1927.

Davidson, George, *Directory for the Pacific Coast of the United States*. Report of the Superintendent of the Coast Survey, U.S. Government, Appendix 44, 1858.

De Voto, Bernard, *The Year of Decision*, 1846. Boston, Little, Brown, 1943.

Dumke, Glenn S., *The Boom of the Eighties in Southern California.* San Marino, Calif., Huntington Library, 1944.

Fink, Augusta, *Time and the Terraced Land.* Berkeley, Calif., Howell-North Books, 1966.

Forbes, Jack D., *Native Americans of California and Nevada.* Healdsburg, Calif., Naturegraph Publishers, 1969.

Fris, Leo J., *Orange County Through Four Centuries.* Santa Ana, Calif., Pioneer Press, 1965.

Gillingham, Robert Cameron, *The Rancho San Pedro.* Los Angeles, Cole-Holmquist Press, 1961.

Gleason, Duncan, *The Islands and Ports of California.* New York, Devin-Adair, 1958.

Griswold, Wesley S., *A Work of Giants.* New York, McGraw-Hill, 1962.

Goodrich, E. P., *Report to Harbor Commission of Los Angeles Concerning the Development and Construction of an Ocean Harbor,* 1913. Los Angeles *Examiner,* 1922.

Guinn, James M., *Historical and Biographical Record of Los Angeles and Vicinity.* Chicago, Chapman Publishing Co., 1902.

Hill, Laurance L., *La Reina: Los Angeles in Three Centuries.* Los Angeles, Security Pacific National Bank, 1929.

Hornbeck, Robert, *Roubidoux's Ranch in the 70's.* Riverside, Calif., Press Printing Co., 1913.

Kraus, George, *High Road to Promontory.* Palo Alto, Calif., American West Publishing Co., 1969.

Layne, J. Gregg, *Annals of Los Angeles.* San Francisco, California Historical Society, 1935.

Lewis, Oscar, *The Big Four.* New York, Knopf, 1938.

————, *California Heritage.* New York, Crowell, 1949.

MacArthur, Mildred Yorba, *Anaheim, "The Mother Colony."* Los Angeles, Ward Ritchie Press, 1959.

McGroarty, John Steven, *History of Los Angeles County.* Chicago, American Historical Society, 1923.

McWilliams, Carey, *Southern California Country.* New York, Duell, Sloan & Pearce, 1946.

Marshall, James, *Santa Fe, The Railroad that Built an Empire.* New York, Random House, 1945.

Matson, Clarence H., *Building a World Gateway.* Los Angeles, Pacific Era Publishers, 1945.

Mayo, Morrow, *Los Angeles.* New York, Knopf, 1932.

1. Marshall, *Santa Fe,* 98.
2. Ibid., 100.

Meadows, Don, *Orange County*. Los Angeles, Dawson's Book Shop, 1966.

Nadeau, Remi, *City-Makers*. Los Angeles, Trans-Anglo Books, 1965.

————, *Los Angeles from Mission to Modern City*. New York, Longman's Green, 1960.

Newmark, Harris, *Sixty Years in Southern California 1853-1913*, 3rd ed. Boston, Houghton Mifflin, 1930.

Newmark, Marco R., *Jottings in Southern California History*. Los Angeles, Ward Ritchie Press, 1955.

Parker, C. E. and Marlyn, *Orange County: Indians to Industry*. Santa Ana, Calif., First American Title Insurance Co., 1963.

Peele, Robert, *Mining Engineers' Handbook*, vol. 1. New York, Wiley, 1941.

Pitt, Leonard, *The Decline of the Californios*. Berkeley, Univ. of California Press, 1970.

Rice, William B., *The Los Angeles Star 1851-1864*. Berkeley, Univ. of California Press, 1947.

Robinson, W. W., *The Changing Scene: A 100 Year Picture-History of Southern California*. Los Angeles, Ward Ritchie Press, 1965.

————, *Los Angeles from the Days of the Pueblo*. San Francisco, California Historical Society, 1959.

————, *Maps of Los Angeles*. Los Angeles, Dawson's Book Shop, 1966.

————, *Panorama: A Picture History of Southern California*. Los Angeles, Title Insurance and Trust Co., 1953.

————, *Ranchos Become Cities*. Pasadena, Calif., San Pasqual Press, 1939.

————, *San Pedro and Wilmington*, Los Angeles, Title Insurance and Trust Company, 1942.

————, *The Story of San Fernando Valley*. Los Angeles, Title Insurance Trust Company, 1961.

Rowland, Leon, *Los Fundadores*. Fresno, Calif., Academy of California Church History, 1951.

Salvator, Ludwig Louis, *Los Angeles in the Sunny Seventies: A Flower from the Golden Land*, orig. ed., 1878. Los Angeles, Jake Zeitlin, 1929.

Sanchez, Nellie VandeGrift, *Spanish Arcadia*. Los Angeles, Powell Publishing Co., 1929.

Stone, Irving, *Men to Match My Mountains*. Garden City, N.Y., Doubleday, 1956.

Swaffield, Roland G., *Saga of the City of Rolling Hills (Old Rolling Hills)*. Long Beach, Calif., Crawford Press, 1958.

Tilden, Freeman, *Following the Frontier*. New York, Knopf, 1964.

Tompkins, Walter A., *Little Giant of Signal Hill*. Englewood Cliffs, N. J., Prentice-Hall, 1964.

Weber, Francis J., *Mission San Fernando*. Los Angeles, Westernlore Press, 1968.

Wharfield, H. B., *Fort Yuma on the Colorado River*. El Cajon, Calif., H. B. Wharfield, 1968.

Willard, Charles Dwight, *The Free Harbor Contest at Los Angeles*. Los Angeles, Kingsley-Barnes & Neuner Co., 1899.

Wilson, Neill C., and Taylor, Frank J., *Southern Pacific*. New York, McGraw-Hill, 1952.

Workman, Boyle, *The City that Grew*. Los Angeles, Southland Publishing Co., 1935.

An Illustrated History of Los Angeles County, California. Chicago, Lewis Publishing Co., Ill., 1889.

1902 Edition of Sears, Roebuck Catalogue. New York, Crown, 1969.

Sears, Spring Through Summer, 1970. Chicago, Sears, Roebuck & Co., 1970.

Gleason, Duncan, "The Lost Islands of San Pedro," *Sea Magazine*, June-August 1951.

Loomis, Charles F., "Making of Los Angeles," *Out West*, Apr. 1909.

Los Angeles *Evening Express*.

Los Angeles *Star*.

Semi-Weekly Southern News (Los Angeles *News*).

Southern Californian.

Index